CALLING THE SHOTS

CALLING THE SHOTS

by Mike Singletary
with Armen Keteyian

CONTEMPORARY
BOOKS, INC.
CHICAGO ▪ NEW YORK

Library of Congress Cataloging-in-Publication Data

Singletary, Mike.
  Calling the shots.

    1. Singletary, Mike.   2. Football players—United
States—Biography.   3. Chicago Bears (Football team)
I. Keteyian, Armen.   II. Title.
GV939.S48A3   1986   796.332'092'4 [B]   86-16549
ISBN 0-8092-4881-6

Published by Contemporary Books, Inc.
180 North Michigan Avenue, Chicago, Illinois 60601
Manufactured in the United States of America
Library of Congress Catalog Card Number: 86-16549
International Standard Book Number: 0-8092-4881-6

Published simultaneously in Canada by Beaverbooks, Ltd.
195 Allstate Parkway, Valleywood Business Park
Markham, Ontario L3R 4T8 Canada

To God, because His blessing allowed me to overcome, through faith and determination, all my shortcomings and gave me the attitude to fight for all the things I have attained.   —*M.S.*

To my wife Dede, daughter Kristen, and my parents Albert and Virginia, for their unwavering support.   —*A.K.*

CONTENTS

FOREWORD

I've made millions of decisions during my coaching career, but saying good-bye to Chicago and Mike Singletary was undoubtedly the most difficult. Sure, in the beginning I yelled at him, called him "Fatso" and "Stupid," grabbing his attention—just like with any other rookie. Mike started off hating me, but as his skills improved, so did our friendship—changing, growing, deepening until one day, I don't remember when, we became father and son.

In this business you resist getting close to players. If you do, they immediately take advantage, stepping past the point of the player-coach relationship and onto your lap. You become a babysitter. But Mike Singletary never crossed that line. Neither did Alan Page or former New York Jet defensive end Gerry Philbin. You could get as close to those men as you wanted and you were always the boss, they were the workers.

A worker. That's Mike Singletary. Without a

doubt, he's the most dedicated athlete I've ever seen. Plenty of football players—quarterbacks mostly—pay lip service to watching film. But they don't watch it like Mike—studying, analyzing, adapting what's on the screen to the game plan. I defy you to run a draw play on him. You can't do it. He's got you scouted so much he knows the play as soon as one back makes a certain move. You can't get that from most players. Hell, half of them aren't smart enough to know what to look for.

But Mike's commitment to excellence and his contribution to the Chicago Bears reach far beyond the film room or the football field. He's the heart and soul of a Super Bowl champion, as big an inspiration off the field as on it. I know for a fact that players on both sides of the ball drew strength from him last year. Coaches, too. He's the reason the Bears will win again this year; I'm not predicting Super Bowl, but Mike just won't let them have a losing season; he's that kind of person. I know I leaned on him, counted on his character more times than I can remember. And believe me, there aren't too many folks in this world you can count on for anything.

Yet Mike's not the only Bear I'm going to miss. I love that defense like it's family. Hell, it *was* family. Hampton. The best defensive tackle in football, a superstar who ended up playing end against my wishes so Fridge could play. Fridge. Now there's a real nice kid. Just not a very good football player, at least at the moment. He's still too heavy. But he's got potential; he might be a good one someday.

Dent. A helluva kid who needed some discipline. I remember having to bench him two years ago because he wouldn't play the trap. But eventually he made All-Pro and led the league in sacks. And he can sure play the trap now.

McMichael. One of the toughest sonofaguns ever

to play the game. He belongs in another era, a time when the players wore high-top shoes and single-bar face masks. He'd pay to play the game.

Fencik and Duerson. Two of the smartest safeties around. Dave really grew up last season, learned to play his help as well as anyone on the squad. And Gary? Well, he's as tough as he is smart, a unique combination since he doesn't have the most natural ability in the world.

Wilber and Otis. A quick prediction on Mr. Marshall: he's going to be a superstar in this league. He learned so quickly, thanks, in part, to Mike Singletary. Two years ago, Wilber didn't know what it took to be a pro; now he's already one of the best linebackers in the game and getting better all the time. Otis? Well, he's just one of the most emotional, intense, fiery players around. Intimidation. That's the game Otis lives to play.

As for my corners, L.A. and Leslie, well, Mike Richardson is still something of a mystery to me, a careless player, great for long stretches, then boom—a silly mistake. Leslie Frazier, on the other hand, is very smart, very steady, with good hands. He's also one of the most unselfish players on the team.

And I guess no good-bye would be complete without saying a word or two about two inspirations on offense, Walter Payton and Jim McMahon. Walter, well, he's just the best running back ever to grace the game. Period. He never wears out, he works, and he does his talking where it counts most—on the football field. McMahon is one guy who isn't intimidated by anything or anybody; he'll take the challenge no matter what or who stands in his way. In that sense, he's a lot like Mike. He lifted our offense to another level every time he stepped onto the field.

Will I miss Mike Ditka? Yes, I guess I will. Sure, we

had our fair share of arguments, mostly when he tried to make defensive suggestions. But he never really told me what to do; I never let him. I said who played, how much, and when. Every now and again, when things weren't going well on the field, Mike would come by and make some suggestions. I'd just tell him to go blank himself, and he'd turn around and walk off. But honestly, I never felt a rift. Maybe Mike did. Maybe he was upset at all the publicity the defense generated, but the way I see it, anything I ever got was the result of how my players played. Ditka and I never had a confrontation; in fact, we hardly ever spoke. I'd just put the game plan on his secretary's desk when I finished it, and she'd put it on his. Not that he understood much of it.

I'm sure all this nonsense will come up again when the Philadelphia Eagles come to Chicago in September to play the Bears. The press is going to have a field day asking about my homecoming, how I'm going to stop McMahon and Walter, my feelings toward Mike. Actually, since it's only the second game of the season—hell, we won't even know our defenses here—what I'd really like to do is trade defenses with Ditka. Mine for his. Even up. He always wanted to play the 3-4 anyway, and that's what they used in Philadelphia last year. He can just borrow my players for the day, and I'll take my defense up there. Might be interesting to see how many points they score. I remember one scrimmage when they went 180 plays without getting into the end zone.

And maybe if I'm lucky, after the game we can pack Mike up and smuggle him back to Philly in an equipment trunk or something. I'd be willing to give up quite a few starters to get him here. But, shit, if the Bears ever let that happen, they'd be in the shithouse real quick.

Finally, I hope Mike and I talk again soon. The last time we spoke was in the locker room right after winning the Super Bowl. We were alone, father and son, in a quiet corner of the coaches' offices. I've called his house a couple of times since and left messages, but I don't think he's ready to talk. But hell, that's OK. He doesn't have to say anything. I know how he feels. I feel the very same way.

Buddy Ryan
Philadelphia, PA
April 4, 1986

Acknowledgments

Many special people have played an important role in my life and career. I'd especially like to thank the following people:

My mom, for all her patience through my sickness and for always taking the time to talk with me;

My brother Grady for the leadership he always tried to show, even when I didn't understand;

Tom Williams, for always being there and for teaching me how to look inside myself;

Oliver Brown, for being the man he is, for instilling in me the importance of pride, and for teaching all the lessons he taught me both in and out of the classroom;

And especially, to my wonderful wife Kim, for her love and encouragment, and for always pushing me to take another step, and my new daughter, Kristin.

Others who deserve special thanks include my family (especially the girls and my brother James), Michael and William Thomas, coach Grant Teaff of

Baylor, coach Corky Nelson, coach Mike Ditka, former Bear teammates Jim Osborne, Revie Sorey, Alan Page, and Bruce Herron; current Bear teammates Brain Cabral, Jimbo Covert, Gary Fencik, Leslie Frazier, Dennis Gentry, Jay Hilgenberg, Wilber Marshall, Steve McMichael, Walter Payton, Dan Rains, Matt Suhey, Cliff Thrift, and Otis Wilson, and to four coaches I'm going to miss, Buddy Ryan, Ted Plumb, Dale Haupt, and Jim LaRue. Also thanks to the inspiration of Norman Vincent Peale, Robert Schuller, and Jimmy Swaggart.

Finally, a great deal of time and effort has gone into the preparation of this book. Thanks are certainly due to Fred Moore, for his persistence and belief in the project, to our editor Shari Lesser for her commitment and editing skills, to our typist Cheryl Pronchick, to *Sports Illustrated*, to John Ware, to Ken Valdiserri of the Bears, and to my collaborator Armen Keteyian for his patience in working with me to bring out feelings I found difficult to discuss.

CALLING THE SHOTS

"I wanted to scream, to hit something, anything, preferably something red and white with a Patriots logo on it. Monsters, even those of the Midway, have feelings too."

1
SATURDAY NIGHT IN NEW ORLEANS

SATURDAY, JANUARY 25, 1986, 11:00 P.M.

Dreams do come true. I was sitting in our final meeting before Super Bowl XX the next day against the New England Patriots. Outside, the city of New Orleans was getting its game face on. Up north, 1,500 miles away, cardinals were rearranging Sunday mass, rabbis were rescheduling wedding ceremonies, and downtown looked like a giant pep rally. The letter *C* shines 10 stories tall outlined on office buildings, TV screens about the size of Soldier Field are set up outside City Hall. And why not? It's only been 8,200 days, 1,198 weeks, or 23 years since the Chicago Bears won a world championship.

At the moment the tight end who starred on that NFL title team was standing in front of the room. We were primed for the Patriots. All we needed was someone to light the fuse.

"I'm not really going to say much," Mike Ditka said. "I'm going to let you guys talk for a change. Gary?"

19

Fencik. Hit man. Bitch. Doom. Articulate graduate of Yale University, reader of Kosinski and Fowles, world traveler, blues freak, fluent in the language of love.

"Sorry, coach, I really don't have anything to share."

"Walter."

The words flowed as smoothly as the man himself. Sweetness, the leading rusher in the history of the National Football League, a living legend.

"The game here is the game I've been trying to get to my entire life," said Walter Payton. "I'm here now, *we're* here now. I just want you guys to know that I'm going to do everything I can to win tomorrow."

"Hampton."

Danimal. The only way to keep this guy out of the lineup is for a doctor to schedule surgery at kickoff. A defensive lineman unlike any other in the NFL.

"You know, guys, I just feel that we gotta get out there and beat the man in front of us and, at the same time, rely on our teammates to do their job. If we do that, there's no reason we can't come away with a victory."

"Coach?"

It was Fencik.

"Well, Coach, I just want to say that for guys like me and Walter who have been around a long time, we never had the pleasure of playing with guys who could build a championship team. It's been a great year, and I just want to let you guys know that I'm going to give all I have tomorrow."

Tears were starting to come to my eyes. Monsters, even those of the midway, have feelings too.

"Samurai."

That's me, defensive co-captain. The man who calls the shots in the Bears huddle. Or, rather, it's part of me. On the field, I project a certain crazed, wild-eyed image. I love to hit, to punish ball carriers. Off the field, I'm just Mike, or Rev, as Derrick Ramsey, the Kentucky tight end I'd be covering tomorrow in the Super Bowl, called me in college— low key, compassionate, committed to making a different impact on others. Either way, I never speak just to hear my own voice. When I speak, you know there's a reason. And because I'm so old-fashioned in my beliefs, I generally dislike nick-names, but in 1983, my third year with the Bears, strong safety Doug Plank hung Samurai on me. (Before that I'd been Chainsaw or the Tasmanian Devil.) Hampton likes Samurai because when I get excited I scream and throw my arms around the way the late John Belushi did on "Saturday Night Live" a few years ago. And I do scream when I hit someone—loud, karate-like yells. And sometimes, when the spirit moves me, I'll pick my victim up, offering a simple "Praise the Lord, brother," with my hand.

"Up to this point we've been playing for everyone else," Samurai said. "We started this season playing for our pride. Then it got to the point where we were playing for the city of Chicago. Then our families. Then Mr. Halas and the coaches. But this time, this one time, let's play it for ourselves. I'm playing this game tomorrow for Walter; I'm playing for Gary, for Otis, for Hampton. I'm playing it for every one of you. I think if we're playing for anyone else, for *anything* else, we're cheating ourselves. If we have anything on our minds other than going out there tomorrow and bringing this victory back to Chicago for the people in this room, who really worked for it, then we're cheating nobody but ourselves."

Well, I don't mind tellin' you, things got a mite crazy after that. Hampton was so fired up he was ready to play right then, in his street clothes. Steve

McMichael, too. We burst out of one room and into another room for defensive meetings. Then Buddy got up to talk. Buddy. Is *love* a four-letter word in the NFL? No? Too bad. Because we love this weather-beaten, foul-mouthed Okie more than words can express.

"Well," said Buddy Ryan, "I just want to let you guys know that I've never been more proud of a defense in my life. And no matter what happens next week, I love you. You'll always be my heroes." Then Buddy sat down.

Next week? What about tomorrow? Was Buddy really leaving the Bears to become an NFL head coach? We'd all heard the rumors; they were filling the newspapers. I looked over at Wilber Marshall, in his second year and already growing into one of the best outside linebackers in the game. It wasn't difficult to read his lips. *Next week?*

"Samurai, Samurai, what have you got to say?"

I sat speechless, rocking back and forth in my chair, mind racing to Buddy, Super Bowl XX, Pats' quarterback Tony Eason, a shot I wanted to put on running back Craig James.

"Samurai?"

"I got nothing to say," I said. "Nothing at all."

"Ah, what the hell," yelled defensive tackle McMichael, alias Mongo and Ming the Merciless. We'd watched about 10 plays on film; Steve had seen enough. He picked up a folding chair and in one swift, violent motion fired it—*vroom*—into a portable blackboard. Ah, scratch one blackboard.

Now defensive line coach Dale Haupt, General Patton with a whistle, is getting fired up, screaming, carrying on. He loves it when we go a little crazy, so he's not above throwing some gas on the fire.

"C'mon, Samurai," my teammates yelled. "C'mon, say something. Go ahead."

I wanted to scream, to hit something, anything, preferably red and white with a Patriots logo on it. "I can't talk, fellas," I said. "Because if I do, we won't have a screen to watch film on anymore."

Suddenly Hampton stood up, all 6'5", 265 pounds of him glaring at the projector. He gave it one quick slap with a huge paw. It dropped like a domino.

"Let's get the hell out of here," he growled.

Chicago, I do believe the wait is over.

"I spent almost all of my life until the age of seven in and out of the hospital. Pneumonia, high blood pressure, oxygen tents, emergency visits to the hospital. Sometimes I was so sick my Mom would just look at me and start crying."

2
GROWING UP

From the outside we appeared an all-American family, a fairy tale come true. My father Charles—Rev we called him—was a preacher man who spread the gospel on street corners in Dallas and other cities in the Southwest before he and my mother, Rudell, settled on Woodward Street in southwest Houston. We lived in a small wood-frame home, sleeping six boys in one room, four girls in another.

The Singletarys. Mom and Dad, Charlie, Jerome, Dale, Dolores, James, Linda, Mary Louise, Grady, Rudell, and me, Michael, the youngest. The center of our universe was not our house, but rather the small white-framed country cottage next door that my father had also built, the Church of God in Christ, where 40 or so faithful would gather on Sunday, huddled together on wooden benches to listen to Reverend Singletary—a large, imposing presence at 6'2", 260 pounds—strum the guitar and preach fire and brimstone. Tambourines would clang, guitars would strum, and folks would shout "Amen" whenever the spirit moved them.

Thinking back, it was like living in the middle of a picture show, one that featured me spending almost all my life until age seven in and out of the hospital. Pneumonia, high blood pressure, oxygen tents, parents getting up in the middle of the night for emergency visits to the hospital. The house, the hospital, and the church were my life; playgrounds, a dream. Sometimes I was so sick my mom would just look at me and start crying. I never drank milk or ate vegetables, junking out instead on candy bars, coffee, or pop, passing time playing cowboys and Indians. I was always the cowboy, the white hat, or Hercules, because he possessed so much power, so much control, the ability to call on the heavens for special help when he needed it.

My dad was a contractor, a six-day-a-week man who, when he wasn't preaching, was pouring concrete and asphalt driveways. All the brothers would work. Well, almost all. Jerome, whom we nicknamed Sonny, would always be off by himself, thinking, talking to some customer, playing their piano or teaching them the latest song. Charles was the most gifted of us all, articulate, inquisitive, leader of the local choir, a beekeeper, as comfortable talking to a doctor as he was to a bum.

My mom, on the other hand, was our role model. She worked every day she could, babysitting two or three other children in our home, ironing clothes, cleaning up houses for contractors, making money scraping paint or puttying windows. That left domestic duties to Dolores, my oldest sister, a great cook but an even better disciplinarian. When Dolores said "one scoop of beans" she meant one. That was it.

With so much activity, so much family interaction, local folks thought we were one of the finest families in Houston. My father was making money, and we seemed happy because when company came over you acted that way—or else.

But my family was living a lie. None of my brothers or sisters really ever talked to my dad. He was too busy attending to others, comforting the sick, the weak, the wicked, to see what was happening in our home. Somebody always needed him more than he thought we did. Mom believed in being there for the kids. But not Dad. He felt that once you got to a certain age you were on your own. He treated us like robots, military men and women, programmed to respond on call—his call. He gave the order, you obeyed, no questions asked—or answered.

Looking back, I guess my dad wasn't prepared for marriage; his mind was filled with everyday needs, feeding and clothing an ever-growing family. The trouble really started when Dale died. He was the third oldest. One night the heater went out, so we brought some coal home to heat the house. Dale was sleeping in the back room with James; Dale was on the end of the bed near the coal-burning stove, James on the other end. About 4:00 A.M., my brother Charles smelled a funny odor—coal fumes coming from the boys' room. I can still remember Charles pounding on the door, crying out for Dale or James to open up. He finally had to run outside and kick the window in. The fumes had suffocated my brother.

Although my parents stayed together after that, it was primarily, I think, for the kids. Because I was so sick, I spent hours at home with my mom, sitting at the kitchen table, talking away the day. Slowly, she taught me the lessons of life, helping me avoid the mistakes my brothers and sisters had made along the way. "Son," she would say, "I just want you to know the only way you're going to make it in life is to treat people the way you want to be treated, to be kind and honest. . . ."

Slowly, my health improved, speeded by my mother's and grandparents' prayers. My grandfather on my mother's side was a Cherokee Indian; my father's dad was German, and his mother was black. My great grandfather on my mother's side was Mexican, and his wife was black. I guess that's what drives me today, my pride in being an American, thinking about my mixed blood, how lucky I was to grow up in a country that would allow people of all cultures, backgrounds, and religions to meet, mate, and make a life of their own. Today I still get very excited about being an American, living in the greatest country in the world, being associated with the finest people in the world. Friends are always telling me I'm the most patriotic person they know. Good. I'm proud to be an American and I want to instill that pride in every person I meet. Where else can a man with my background, my heritage, grow up to be the best? And that's what I want to be. The best student, best father, best Christian, best football player. That's my single motivation in life, being the best.

It was shortly after Dale's death that I realized my dad was drifting away. It was beginning to be more and more difficult to watch him preach on Sundays, control an audience, spreading the word, knowing he was exposing himself to another side of life. There were temptations in my father's life, and he accepted them.

Grady sensed the drift, and because he knew those ropes, he did his best to make sure his little brother never got tangled up in them. By now, I had recovered enough to play outside more and expand my circle of friends. Many times Ron Williams, still my best friend today, and I would head off to

Sunnyside Park where we'd pal around, playing basketball. A lot of my peer group were drinking beer and smoking cigarettes—even in the fourth grade—but Grady was forever chiding me "I don't ever want to see you smoking" as he puffed on a cigarette, or "I don't ever want to see you drinking" as he drank one himself. With Grady it wasn't brother-brother but father-son, filling the void created when my dad moved out, to the other side of town, to a bigger house, to another woman. Oh, dad still stopped by every morning to pick up the boys for work. And when he left my mom would just sit in the kitchen and cry. "Don't worry, mom," I would say. "One of these days I'm going to buy you a big new house."

Before my dad moved out, he allowed me to try out for football. Originally, he was dead set against it; he really didn't understand the need for competition. None of my brothers or sisters played sports; the only member of our family who was into athletics was my cousin Greg, a Golden Gloves champion in Dallas. Competition for us arrived when some neighborhood tough picked on one of us because we *didn't* participate. My father's answer to that was to pile all six boys into the pickup and make a house call on the bully. Kids quickly found out, if you fought one Singletary, you fought us all. Still, the fire was burning inside me, stoked every Sunday as I'd sit glued to the TV set, six inches away from the screen, watching my Cowboy heroes—Roger Staubach, Bob Lilly, LeRoy Jordan—plant the seeds of America's Team.

At 5'2", 130 pounds, I was the smallest kid in the seventh grade who tried out for football, having lied to Coach Miller, telling him my father had allowed me to try out, just to warrant a suit. "Well, you better take this form home and have your parents sign it," said Miller. He'd eyed my growing athletic skills in gym class, watched me toss the ball around. He got to calling me "Suitcase" because I always carried around a black bag with my notes, "I think you're going a lot of places in life," he'd tell me.

"Sign these papers, will ya, Dad?" I said.

"Let me read them first."

"It's nothing," I said. "Just some stuff from school."

He read them anyway; so did Mom, quickly deciding she wanted no part of her son's dismemberment. "You're just getting healthy," she said. "Well," answered my dad, "I'll tell you what. If you play well enough in the first game—and I'll be over there watching you—then I'll let you play. But if you don't play well, you're not going to play. You're going to work for me and that's it."

My mom refused to submit. She wanted no more hospital time for her youngest child. But my father surprised me. "Let him play," he said. "We've prayed so much already and he's done well." He signed the consent form.

Friday arrived, game day, but Dad never showed. Grady was there, though, watching with me from the sidelines. I was a reserve linebacker on the junior varsity, getting steamrolled something like 25-0. The fourth quarter started, and I still hadn't set foot on the field. My brother kept looking at me, wondering if this was what I meant by playing football. He didn't understand much, and at this point I wasn't about to offer any explanations.

Finally, my linebacker coach, Coach Cunningham, had seen enough.

"Suitcase."

"Yes, sir!"

"Get in there."

My legs were shaking. The first play was a trap; a cavernous hole opened wherein I was greeted by the sight of the largest human being I'd ever seen in my life. As the fullback ran straight at me I took the only sensible course—I ducked, throwing my hands in the air. He rambled over my body and into the end zone for six points.

Grady just shook his head as I jogged off the field. I played a couple more downs, then the game mercifully ended. I figured my career—and life—were over; I was destined to 30 years of backbreaking labor, pouring concrete and laying asphalt driveways.

"Well, Singletary," said my coach, "at least you went in there when I yelled. A lot of guys wouldn't have even done that."

I turned to my brother. "What are you going to tell Dad?" I asked.

Grady smiled. "I'm just going to tell him you did the best you could."

From that moment on, football was a joy to me. Summer arrived and so did my appetite. I ate everything in sight, loading up on bread, drinking a gallon of milk a day. Coffee and candy were out. In no time I grew six inches, to 5'8", and added 20 pounds. I needed that strength because that summer, when I was 12, my parents finally divorced. Really, it was more a relief than anything else; we'd been living in constant turmoil for years.

My father's absence—he'd moved out when I was 10—made inevitable my ascension into class clown. I was a rebellious, smart-alecky sort who questioned the simplest chores, even taking out the garbage. And every time it was Grady who corrected me. "You'll get it now," he said. I got it now.

Most of my afternoons were spent in Sunnyside Park playing basketball and contemplating life. I do, however, remember one special day, speaking with Grady as he sat in the front seat of his shiny blue Malibu, a car he kept so spotless you could use the hood as a shaving mirror. Grady was very cool, a

real ladies' man and, at 22, on the cutting edge of
every trend. If a new hairstyle came out, he was the
first to try it. The same for clothes and even more
intimate things, like drugs. On this day he just sat in
the car, looking at me. "Always, whatever you do, do
your best," he said. He reached into his pocket and
pulled out a couple of bucks. "Buy yourself a pop or
something," he said, and I started to walk away.

"Mike."

I turned around.

"Remember what I told you. Do your best. And
mind your mom."

Two days later Grady was dead. He'd been driving
out of Houston toward Arcola when he innocently
got involved in a six-car traffic accident caused by a
drunk driver—the only one who lived. The phone
rang around midnight, someone from the hospital
telling us Grady was hurt—nothing serious, despite
the news that his car had flipped. But would we
mind coming down anyway. Well, it was serious. A
blood clot had formed on Grady's brain. But the
doctors assured us he was out of danger. "He's
young and strong," they said. "No need to wait." We
went home in paralyzed relief. The next day,
another call. Grady was dead.

Thinking about it today, it's hard to express the
shock of losing another brother, just months after
seeing my father walk out of my life forever.
Grady's death was devastating; it knocked the family completely off balance; it tipped the domestic
scales for good, spreading the family all over the
map, leaving me and Mom alone most of the time. I
was forced to make some quick decisions, the biggest of my life. I vowed to take care of my mom, to
buckle down in school and start studying, to do
what Grady had asked of me.

The next year I made all-district linebacker; the
following season, when I was in ninth grade, I was an

all-city offensive guard and an all-conference line-backer. I ran track. But since we didn't even have a field events coach, I went to the library and checked out a book by former world record holder Randy Matson. I loved to read—particularly NFL books about great linebackers and defensive teams—Butkus, Nitschke, Lanier, the Purple People Eaters in Minnesota. Matson wrote about the importance of speed, velocity, and power, relating it to a knockout punch in boxing. Through his writings I learned the techniques I use today in making explosive hits on running backs and wide receivers. You have to be a striker, to explode at contact, flowing through the chest, driving up and through the back. The resultant feeling has always been almost indescribable to me, akin to being struck, I suppose, by a bolt of lightning—a blast that, for one brief second, shines through your mind and body like a flash of brilliant white heat.

And even though football took more and more of my time, I had hardly anyone to share it with. Grady was gone; my dad had his own life. Finally, my sister, Mary Louise, the third oldest girl, got married to a young man named Michael Thomas, a very enthusiastic sports fan. Michael was a paraplegic (my sister was a nurse). So, from seventh grade through my senior year in high school, Michael came to every game, rain or shine, always with a smile on his face. Soon others followed, especially in high school after they read my name in the papers. My mom, my sister Linda, her husband Bill, Willie, and Rudell all became regulars.

Worthing High School, one of the few all-black high schools left in Houston, is a flat, two-story, nondescript brick building, distinguished perhaps by the fact that in 30-odd years of education, it's remained clean and remarkably graffiti-free. Worthing has been home to some of the finest track

athletes in Texas high school history—names like
Otis Taylor, who went on to become an All-Pro
receiver for the Kansas City Chiefs; Los Angeles
Raiders wide receiver Cliff Branch; Kenneth Curl,
the first 9.3 100-yard dash man; Carl Douglas, a
shotputter who became the first black quarterback
to play in the NFL (he backed up Johnny Unitas in
Baltimore); and Olympic sprinter Deborah Ed-
wards. Yes, Worthing had tremendous pride in its
track program. Football, however, was another
story—a sad one at that. The team had never made
the playoffs. Still, Worthing was a place where
teachers' lessons reached beyond the classroom,
the talk touching on the importance of making your
mark in life. And nobody delivered that message
more strongly or with more feeling than Oliver
Brown, the school's indomitable track and football
coach and math teacher. Coach Brown was a big
man who carried an even bigger stick. No one
messed with bad, bad, Oliver Brown.

By the time I entered Worthing I had established
something of a reputation for myself as a football
player. I was now 5'10", 180 pounds, and packed a
pretty big wallop. I'll never forget my first day in
high school, filling out my class schedule, when
Coach Brown strolled over. At the time, I wasn't
interested in taking academic risks. My goal was to
stay eligible, to stick with the basics in math and
English. Until Coach Brown asked me to show him
my schedule, that is.

"What the heck is this?" he said. "You're not going
to play middle linebacker for me with a schedule
like that." Then he gave me a speech I'll never
forget: "Always remember, Michael, the easiest way
out is the worst way to go. Anything worth having is
worth working for. If you make an A in Fundamental Math here, what did you gain? Nothing, that's
what. You know you can do that. So I'm going to put

you down for an algebra course, Algebra II, in fact. Now, if you make a D in this class, you've still done more than getting an A in Fundamental."

He gave me a long, hard look. "Remember, son, don't take any shortcuts."

As time went on, as I found out more and more about this Oliver Brown's unique capacity to analyze and motivate athletes. He quickly became a major influence in my life, filling the void of a fatherlike figure. "Look at that track there," he told me one day. "It will tell you a lot about yourself. See that guy over there? He's a dog. He doesn't want to work. And over there, that guy hiding behind the bushes. When he gets back over here, I'm just going to tell him to do it all again. It's either going to make him or break him. . . . There are two things in life. One is to be able to communicate—don't ever walk around and not be able to express yourself. The other is math. You can't replace it."

Well, I got that D in Algebra II, and Coach Brown beat me to death about it, too. "Take it again," he said. So I took it again. This time, I earned a B. He still beat on me, just as he did when I got an A. "Why didn't you get an A-plus?" he'd say. But that was just his style. No one ever complained. At least Coach Brown cared. So did I. Geometry, trigonometry, and calculus soon followed. By the time I left Worthing, I wanted to major in math.

In the meantime, I was continuing to grow as an athlete, lifting weights almost daily in my garage. The place eventually attracted neighborhood kids— guys twice my age—and even the high school basketball coach started sending players over. Yet because my size was a question, during my senior year I wasn't exactly deluged with college offers. It also didn't help matters much that the team wasn't heavily scouted, and the papers paid us scant attention. I can still remember referees telling me,

"You're a great football player, kid; we've got to find a way to get you out of here." Despite such hardships, I finished the third-highest-rated linebacker in the state that year, my size (I'm 5'11½") keeping most major colleges off my doorstep—despite some fervent prayers. Home life was still a tangled mess. My dad had now remarried and run into problems with Uncle Sam and my mom couldn't afford to send me. "Lord," I said, "if you want me to play college football, show me a sign."

Baylor assistant coach Ron Harms wasn't wearing any signs when he showed up to scout an All-American fullback for Lamar High School, one of our conference opponents, but it didn't matter. He liked what he saw in me, taking some film home to head coach Grant Teaff who, I'm told, watched two, maybe three defensive series before telling Harms to offer me a scholarship. Hard to believe, but at the time I didn't know what a scholarship was. Coach Brown kept telling me I might get one, and I'd say, "That's nice, that's a nice honor," thinking it was some kind of award or something.

Sure enough, Harms talked to me about a scholarship—not that I knew yet what he was offering. But I liked him, how he related to black athletes and that he never offered anything illegal, unlike other schools. I would soon get into situations where friends would say they'd signed at one college or another, telling me, "Mike, you can sign, too, and we'll both get cars." That wasn't my style; my mom and Coach Brown wouldn't have stood for it. "Never get yourself obligated to anyone," my mom always said.

Baylor University is nestled along the banks of Texas's Brazos River in the city of Waco, halfway between the capital city of Austin and the Dallas–Fort Worth Metroplex area. One of the first recruits

I met on my visit was a player from Houston named Thomas Earl Young. "Man, I ain't coming here," Thomas said, realizing perhaps that Baylor is the largest Baptist university in the world. "Ain't no way I'm coming here."

"You have another scholarship?" I said.

"Yeah," said Thomas Earl. "I think I'm going to Nebraska, Mike."

"Really? What kind of scholarship do they give you?"

Thomas Earl looked at me as though I had just sprouted wings. "The same kind of scholarship I'm getting here," he said. "We don't have to pay for nothing for four years." About this time, we walked into the athletic cafeteria. Fresh milk, all the food you could eat, and books and tuition, too. I was hooked, even more so after meeting Grant Teaff.

Coach Teaff was seen as something of a savior at the time, and for good reason. Prior to 1972, Baylor hadn't won a Southwest Conference title in nearly 50 years, a frustration multiplied tenfold by the team's history of 20 second- or third-place finishes. But after Coach Teaff was hired, his open charismatic manner, humble attitude, and tireless work habits began winning more than just football games. I relished the fact that he spoke openly of accepting God as a 12-year-old in Snyder, Texas, how it had helped him adjust to some personal tragedies. Sure, he'd won conference titles and achieved some remarkable success as a coach, but he also nearly died when a plane carrying the team from McMurry College in Abilene, where he was a young head coach, was forced to make four emergency landings one night, the final time with the right engine in flames. He had also witnessed a player paralyzed for life after sustaining a neck injury in a game, and another of his athletes had died of cancer. He'd also suffered in silence when his daughter, Tammy, was diagnosed as having multiple sclerosis. But Coach Teaff always fought back; today he has written two books about the importance of believing and winning. Not the winning associated with scoreboards but, rather, the kind that means overcoming odds, taking adversity and body-slamming it to the turf. That's the kind of coach and man I wanted to play for, despite a fine visit to the University of Texas, in Austin, where the Longhorns rolled out the welcome mat. But in the end I didn't get the same feeling about Austin as I did for Waco and Coach Teaff. When he called and asked what I thought, I told him he had himself a linebacker. Harms and a host of Baylor alums arrived at my house the following day to sign the papers.

Everybody was there—my mom, sisters, brothers—everyone except my dad. Swallowing that pill wasn't easy, but I'd taken the same medicine a few weeks earlier when Worthing played its first game in the Astrodome. I called my dad to offer a special invitation; he promised he'd be there. When I saw him the next day at work on Saturday, I knew right away from the way he answered my questions he'd never watched the game. Looking back, I understand he was busy building another life, but it didn't make it any easier for me to understand. At the time I hated him. I felt he didn't care about our family, and we were quickly losing whatever feelings we had left for him.

Again, Coach Brown found the right words to ease the pain, speaking as the father I'd long since lost. He stopped me one day in front of the gym, late in my senior year. "Mike," he said, "I want you to understand something. You've just stepped to another plateau. What are you going to do? A lot of guys get there, and the next thing you know, you turn around, and they're right back here again, making excuses. Don't do that. Always remember, the minute your step starts getting slow, somebody's catching up. When you're at Baylor, don't think of anything but your work first. Go out on that field and go for it. Don't settle for second best. Do what you gotta do, keep working hard. And I don't care how good somebody is telling you you're getting—don't settle for it. Always try to get better."

"Kansas City called, advising me it was down to just me and Willie Scott. They took Scott. Chicago was next: 'It's between you and Keith Van Horne.' They took Van Horne. When Los Angeles selected Mel Owens, a 6'2" 224-pound linebacker, I stopped caring."

"There may have been players who hit harder, who tackled better, who ran faster, who were smarter, stronger, or read coverage better. But collectively, nobody did it better than Mike Singletary. And I don't think anyone in the Southwest Conference ever has."
                    —Baylor coach Grant Teaff

3
BAYLOR

It had to be an optical illusion. But there it was. Singletary. Last on the list. Unlucky number 13.

I walked over to assistant coach Corky Nelson's office. It was the spring of my freshman year in Texas. I'd met Coach Nelson, the linebacker coach, upon my arrival at Baylor. "We've got two pretty good linebackers in the middle already," he had said. "You're going to have to wait your turn. You'll get a fair chance."

Well, I waited until the first scrimmage. Our offensive line was big, tough, and feeling their oats, getting off on bullying the freshmen, whom they capriciously knocked around during scrimmages. That's fine off the field. If a senior wants to embarrass me off the field, to include me in a little friendly hazing, fine. But not on the field. That's different. That's my time. We're equals.

In practice, I know only one speed—full. I don't say much (I didn't speak 20 words my first 1½ years

41

on the team), but I hit everything and anything that moved. My first day I was so intense, conducting warm-ups at full speed, that one of the linemen, a hulk named Sledge, got ticked off. "What's your problem?" he complained. "Trying to be an All-American or something?" I looked him straight in the face, and, if I may say so, his mug had a certain similarity to that of a bulldog. I looked him straight in the eye, intense, so much so, I swear he could hear me speak under my breath: "Yes," I said, "as a matter of fact, I am."

Eight games into my freshman year I started. The team had been playing a standard 5-2 defense and lost some close games. So, before Arkansas in number eight, Coach Teaff switched to a 4-3 and put me in the lineup. I responded with 28 unassisted tackles. By the end of the year, I was the league's "newcomer of the year" and honorable mention All-Conference. But, at the same time, I was still having problems controlling myself, regulating my breathing on the field. (I had a tendency to hyperventilate.) In high school I had calmed down some by listening to Bach and Beethoven before a game, but at Baylor even the Masters weren't helping, and team trainer Skip Cox was concerned. "Son, you're going to have to realize you can't go on like this," he told me. "You're going to have to settle down. You can be a great football player, but at this pace you'll wear yourself out."

Taking the trainer's advice, I started off slowly in spring practice my sophomore year. After one of the first scrimmages Nelson shouted me over. "Something's wrong," he said. "I don't know what it is, but something is wrong. It's not you out there. You can be the greatest linebacker who ever played, but you're not going to do it like this."

"Wait a minute," I said. "I talked to Cox, and he told me to slow down."

"Not while you play," Nelson explained. "You have to know when to turn it on and turn it off. Until you get that, you're going to have problems."

Great! To top it off, the trainer is telling me to ride a stationary bike five miles a day to build up my stamina, and I'm dying after 1½. "You've got to find your pace," said Cox. "You can't go full-blast for five miles." So I eased off, went with the flow, and felt better.

Spring practice ended. The list went up. No. 13. We had a meeting in Coach Nelson's office. All the linebackers were there, Nelson praising each one until he got to my name. "Singletary, you stink!" he roared. "That's right, stink!" He was right in my face; I could feel his breath. "You always want to do what *you* want to do." I was crying, tears streaming down my cheeks. Inside I wanted to scream, to hit someone. Then Nelson said, "Until you start doing things my way, you're not going to play." He completed the thought with an irate "Do you understand me?"

I couldn't understand what I'd done. I lost it. "I don't care what you do. I don't even want to be a starter here." I was working hard both on and off the field. I had changed my major from premed (I had wanted to be a physical therapist to help Michael Thomas walk again) to business administration and broadcasting because the academic load was just too much. But I was still putting in the hours, both on and off the field. I got up from the chair and walked toward the door. "I hate you," I said, spitting out the words. "I don't care if I ever start or ever play again at this school." I slammed the door on my way out.

He started to scream. "Hey, you sonofagun, get back in here! Don't ever walk out on me! You earn the right to start around here, and until you do, you're going to stay right where you are." By this time, he was so close to me he almost touched my lips.

I realize now that Coach Nelson was crazy enough to pick me up and toss me back through that door. He is a wild man, certifiably crazy; he doesn't care if you are seven feet tall and weigh 500 pounds; when he dies, he dies. That's his philosophy. He's head coach at North Texas State now, and I'm sure he's given his players the same speech he gave to me. "You'll do what I say, when I say it, and how I say it," he said. The look in his eyes pulled me back into the center of the room. "Yes," I said. His voice and eyes quickly softened at the same time. "Mike, I see something in you that I think is really special. But you're not going to do it by taking shortcuts or trying your own way all the time. You've got to do it our way."

He was right. There was no question about the effectiveness of my helmet-cracking hitting style (I would break 16 of those suckers in four years, all my own, all lined up in a row in the equipment room), but my technique was second-rate. I crossed my feet on pass coverage; I overran sweeps. "You have to learn to read plays," Nelson said. "You can't just go in there and tear things up. You can knock anybody down, but that's not going to do us any good if the back is running 30 or 40 yards downfield."

I began to grow. I did it Coach Nelson's way during spring ball, and by the time of our season opener against Georgia my sophomore year, I was ready to go, so much so, that in one play against the Bulldogs I busted up a two-man block on a short pass and crashed into the ball carrier, Willie McClendon, without my helmet. By the end of the year, I had broken the school's single-season record for tackles (I had 232 in 11 games) and was named Defensive Player of the Year in the Southwest Conference. My junior year I was named tri-captain, we won eight games, played Clemson in the Peach Bowl, and I won the prestigious Davey O'Brien award. Again, I was selected Player of the Year in the conference. My senior year I repeated as conference MVP—the only three-time defensive winner in history—won the Davey O'Brien award again, was runner-up for the Lombardi award, annually given to the nation's outstanding "linemen," top 10 in the Heisman balloting, and a consensus first team All-American for the second straight year. In four years I had averaged 15 tackles per game, never had fewer than 10 in any game, and collected 30 or more on three different occasions.

Thinking back, the war game was always Baylor–SMU. The Mustangs had the Pony Express of Craig James and Eric Dickerson, but what really made the rivalry special were the tremendous comebacks we staged against one another. My sophomore year we led SMU 28-0 but lost 32–28. The next year it was SMU 21-0 before they lost 28–21. The exact same thing happened my senior year, 28–21 Baylor. That year, Eric ran the ends and Craig rammed it up the middle. One time I saw Eric, smooth as silk, break outside and meet our rugged safety head on; Eric barely broke stride, running right over the guy. I felt then, as I do now, that he's one of the best running backs I've ever seen in my life.

Because of my achievements and notoriety, I figured I'd be a first-round draft choice. After all, hadn't I proved to the scouts that I could play? So what if I traveled to two postseason All-Star games (in Japan and Hawaii), ignoring pressure from pro scouts to attend the Senior Bowl in Mobile, Alabama. To me, that game represented computer drafting at its best (or worst): the measuring, testing, probing, analyzing of everything except a player's heart.

Since I knew I was a first-round draft pick, I continued making speeches, the banquet circuit bringing my weight above 240. Then, all of a sudden, I started hearing about how great this guy Lawrence Taylor was; people, scouts were putting him in a class above Hugh Green of Pittsburgh, who I knew would go first-round. I know it's hard to believe now, but I'd never heard of Taylor. Soon, even more new names were surfacing, size guys, compu-picks. It was getting ridiculous.

Then Jim Parmer, a Chicago scout, visited me. "Singletary," he said, "I've looked at your films, and you're just what we need in Chicago. I like your style, and you're pretty rugged." I said, "Well, what do you think?" He said, "First or second round, we're going to be looking for you." "Don't wait for the second round," I told Parmer. "I'm not going to be there."

Parmer concluded the conversation by telling me it was between me and an offensive tackle. Before he left I made sure he knew where I stood. "Don't wait for the second round," I insisted. "I'm not going to be there. And remember just one thing: if you do draft me, I'm going to be the greatest linebacker in history. That's the greatest of all time. Don't forget it."

That may sound conceited, but I honestly wasn't thinking anything about second round or second best. I expressed that feeling to every club that called me. When draft day arrived, however, my confidence cracked like one of those 16 helmets. One by one, a star-studded group of college seniors, future NFL all-pros—George Rogers, Taylor, Freeman McNeil, Kenny Easley, Ronnie Lott—heard their names called. Me? I kept waiting.

Then Kansas City called, Worthing alum Otis Taylor advising me it was down to just me and wide receiver Willie Scott. They took Scott. Chicago was next: "It's between you and Keith Van Horne of USC," they told me. They took Keith. When Los Angeles selected Mel Owens of Michigan, a 6'2", 224-pound linebacker, I stopped caring. *Mel Owens.* I barely heard the rest of the round . . . Dennis Smith . . . Mark Nichols . . . Marion Barber . . . John Harty. I could have gone in the 100th round; it didn't matter now. I wasn't going to play. I was a victim of some conspiracy, beaten by a cold, computerized game. I walked outside the hotel in Houston where I had been monitoring the draft. I needed some air, a place to think. My girlfriend and future wife, Kim, tried to ease my bitterness, but I pulled away, walking the parking lot, alone, angry. "Lord," I said, "only You know what's best. If You want me to play this game, give me a sign. The only team I want to play for is Chicago."

Not one minute later I heard a voice calling my name.

"Mike, Mike!"

I turned around to see both Kim and her mother.

"Mike," Kim yelled across the lot, "they just announced that Chicago has made some trade with San Francisco to move up in the draft. The Bears picked you on the second round."

*"Buddy never let up on me: Do this. Do that. You're fat. You're slow. You're stupid. You're fat, slow, **and** stupid. I'd beg him during a game to let me play, and he'd give me his grandfatherly smile and say 'Naw, rookie, you'd better stay over here with me. We want to win this one.' "*

*"Buddy never remembers anyone's name. Mike got
called '50' a lot. But one thing was clear. Mike liked
to hit people. The only question was whether he
would learn the system and pass coverage. But he
definitely liked to hit. He was, and still is, in a
class by himself. Nobody made noises like he does.
Grunts, groans . . . he sounded like a kamikaze."*
—Alan Page, Chicago Bear, 1978–82

4
BEARING UP
The Early Years—or "Hey, 50, Get Your Fat Ass Over Here."

As a business major, I'd always questioned the need
for agents, particularly after college experiences of
being wooed with sleazy promises of cash, cars, and
women if I would sign with certain "big name"
agents. Instead of one of the hotshot agents, I chose
an Oriental kid from Abilene named Jim Bob Bird to
represent me. I told Jim Bob during my junior year
I wanted his help; I trusted him and I felt that he
was intelligent enough to handle my contract
negotiations.

Jim Bob was smart enough, all right, but I quickly
discovered his inexperience really hurt. Naturally, I
was his first client, and he was pitted against Bears
general manager Jim Finks, the man responsible for
drafting Hampton, Otis Wilson, Matt Suhey, and for
signing Fencik, McMichael, Leslie Frazier, and Jay
Hilgenberg, among others, as free agents. Finks had
also been on the firing line at Minnesota for years
before Chicago, and he had earned a well-deserved

reputation for being a very class guy, but a hard-nosed, bottom-line negotiator.

We had trouble right off the bat. I wanted first-round money, whether I had been drafted in the second or sixth round. To me, that meant three years, $120,000. Well, during the summer of 1981, I got Finks's offer: $22,000 for one year. "It's just a ploy," a friend told me, a tactic; but tactic or not, I wouldn't sign. I forced Finks to come to Houston, where we met in a barbecue restaurant owned by Tom Williams, one of my closest friends, who happens to have one of the finest football minds in the game. Tom was an assistant head coach and defensive coordinator for the legendary Eddie Robinson at Grambling from 1956–66 before becoming the first black assistant general manager in the NFL when he worked for Houston from 1966 to 1977. In addition to the restaurant, Williams ran a place called Coaches, a fitness center specializing in rehabilitation, conditioning, and technique training for pro athletes. We'd known each other since my junior year at Baylor, and he would soon play a greater role in my life.

Well, the meeting didn't last long. Jim Bob was trying to drive a hard bargain, but I could see dead-end signs straight ahead. Finally, I got mad. "If you can't get me these numbers, then forget it," I said, walking out. Well, Jim Bob couldn't get them, and in retrospect, it was silly and foolish for me even to ask him to try. Finks was just too experienced. But, actually, the negotiating was a blessing in disguise. I got a better deal than a rookie might expect, even though my friendship with Jim Bob eventually broke up over his inexperience in money management. Like a lot of first-year players, I'd asked my agent to manage my money and pay my monthly bills because I didn't want to be bothered with it. But then I got into a couple of business deals that went sour. Suddenly someone is telling you, "Well, we lost $5,000," when the "we" was actually *me*. I began to handle my own money, feeling the necessity of planning for my family's future. I learned to invest on my own, learning from my experience with Jim Bob that prudence and prosperity often go hand in hand.

Because of my protracted contract squabble I missed the first three days of training camp. I had envisioned Chicago as a city full of steel mills and smog. Instead, I saw glistening towers, landmark architecture, the Loop, North Side mansions, and high-rise luxury apartments. Strangely, it was particularly cold for July . . . and windy. I knew the club's football history like my Baylor playbook, how the team dated back to September 17, 1920, when the old American Football Association was formed in Canton, Ohio, when the league "owners" held their first meeting on the running boards of cars in an auto showroom. I knew it was a team with unparalleled tradition, a history filled with colorful, contentious players like Red Grange, Bulldog Turner, Cash & Carry Pyle, George McAfee, Bill George, Doug Atkins, Sid Luckman, Bronko Nagurski, Dick Butkus, and Gale Sayers. I wanted so badly to be a magical, mystical Monster of the Midway, an indirect descendant of the great Papa Bear himself, George Halas. True, the Bears weren't so great anymore; the team had won its last title in 1963, and managed only two winning seasons in the last 13, since Halas himself retired from coaching. The year before, in 1979, the Bears had lost nine games.

On my first day as a Bear, head coach Neill Armstrong introduced himself by ordering me to do grass drills, "up-downs," in the mud. Yet it did nothing to remove the chip on my shoulder, the one I'd set up there after being snubbed in the draft. My

competition was Tom Hicks of Illinois, a five-year
veteran and starter, and Lee Kunz of Nebraska.
Hicks was holding out, upset over the contract I'd
signed; he would not play for less money than a
rookie.

Team headquarters, as any Bear fan knows, are in
the city of Lake Forest, on the campus of Lake
Forest College, an old-moneyed area of Tudor mansions and tree-lined streets, the setting for the film
Ordinary People. We practice on two different
fields: one directly behind Halas Hall, the three-
story brick building erected in honor of Papa Bear
in 1979, and the other across the street on the
practice facility of the Lake Forest Foresters. After
I finished the up-downs, I was breathing hard as I
ran over to the defensive huddle, where I noticed a
short, stubby, fat coach wearing a T-shirt, shorts,
and a Bears cap. He looked like a farmer, not a
football coach. "Hey, 50," he said, "let's see if you're
in shape. Run some gases. Sideline to sideline, over
and back, over and back, and make sure your feet
touch the line." He watched me endure this torture
for about five minutes. He couldn't contain his glee.
"Ah, yeah, you fat little rascal," he cried, "you're out
of shape. You're nothing, 50, nothing; just a short
little fat guy."

Welcome to the world of Buddy Ryan. Soon it was
another order: "Hey, 50," he yelled, "get your fat ass
over here and do this." *This* was the 880 time trial
I'd missed during my holdout. I was just about to
say something when Jerry Muckensturm, a veteran
linebacker, spoke up. "Singletary, you're just what
we need around here." I got so excited by those
words I took off scared to death (the entire team
was watching), like a thoroughbred running six
furlongs. Unfortunately, this was distance running,
and after leading on the first lap, I died on the
backstretch.

The next day I had to run again; the time to break was 2:30. As team trainer Fred Caito was taping me up, I asked him, "Hey, Fred, did you ever know anyone who couldn't run long distance?" "Yeah," he said, "Jimmy Brown hated it." "Well, why can't Buddy understand that?" "Ah, don't worry," Fred said. "Just go out and do the best you can." So I took Fred's advice, jogging the first 440, figuring Ryan wasn't serious. Wrong. "You dog, you don't have an ounce of pride in you!" he screamed. He was talking out of the side of his mouth, biting off the words.

Now I was getting pissed off. At the annual Bear scrimmage I'd been busting heads all over the place, growling, yelling, and Armstrong loved it, telling reporters with a wry grin how he liked my "personality change." They'd waived Hicks that same day, so I must be doing something right. But here's this Okie calling me names. Nobody calls me a dog. Nobody says I have no pride. Nobody.

"What time do you get up in the morning?" I asked Buddy.

He said, "Seven, eight. Why? What's on your mind?"

"I'm going to run this thing tomorrow, and I'm going to do it on time if it kills me."

"All right, all right, I'll be here," Ryan said, giving me a quizzical look. "Just make sure you're here on time."

I couldn't sleep all night, tossing, turning, praying, asking for the strength to get through what I imagined would be the longest two minutes and thirty seconds of my life. When I saw Buddy the next morning, bright and early, I asked if he was a Christian. "Yeah," he grumbled, "I teach Sunday school." I asked what church. "Don't worry about it." The growl got louder. He pulled a stopwatch from his back pocket. "Let's get going here."

I never felt a thing. I wasn't even breathing hard

when I finished. "It's about time," Buddy mumbled, shuffling away. Just then, Armstrong appeared. "You made it, huh, Mike?" he said. I told him I finally stopped trying to do it alone. "I know what you mean," said Armstrong. "I know what you mean."

Looking back, I guess part of Neill's problem was that he cared too much, wanted to be too close to his players, their family life. He is a good man, a great man, and a solid, if uninspiring football coach. The trouble was, the team just took advantage of his good heart and began missing meetings, disobeying orders. Sure, the 1981 draft had brought in some terrific talent—Van Horne, Ken Margerum from Stanford, Todd Bell of Ohio State, and Jeff Fisher—but very few veterans, less than half the football team, had a commitment to win. Most were more concerned about radio shows and their love lives than the Bears. Time after time, Todd and I would run after practice, and some of the older guys would laugh, chiding us that it was too cold, calling us crazy. They never understood the best opportunities come from winning. That's why people want you. They had no priorities.

Todd Bell and I drew close from the start. Like me, he was the son of a Pentecostal minister, and had come from a big family. He also happened to be an All-American linebacker in high school in Ohio, an accomplishment he never let me forget. "Mike, ever make All-American in high school?" he'd always ask me, a smile on his face. A great track star, Todd had won the long jump three years running in Ohio, breaking Jesse Owens's 1933 record when he ran a 9.7 100. Still, in 1980, he was two years away from starting full-time, making his mark now on special teams. We always sat together at meetings, drawing strength to endure Buddy's abuse. By this time, Buddy had taken to calling Todd "Taco" and me "Fat Jap."

Once Hicks was cut, I assumed I would start, backed up by Kunz. That's what happened in the first two exhibition games, but I quickly realized that the pros were a world apart from the college game. Coming from the Southwest Conference, I'd been taught to concentrate on the quarterback and the backs, and 90 percent of the time you'd find the football. That wasn't the case in the pass-happy pros. I couldn't read the linemen. Worse, I wasn't excited about playing the passing teams—San Diego, Kansas City, Miami. I wanted to blast the ball carrier. The least little fake and I'd be into the line, and the tight end, my responsibility, would be running free downfield. When that happened much more than it should, I sat down and Kunz took over.

I stayed seated until the final preseason game. Finally, I couldn't stand it anymore. I ran up to Buddy and said, "Let me go in there, let me go in there." Buddy gave me his grandfatherly smile and said, "Naw, rookie, you'd better stay over here with me. We want to win this one."

I could have KO'd him right there. One shot. I called Kim and told her how much I hated him. I didn't know whether to hang it up or suck it up. What kept me sane was talking with Todd about the disappointments. "You know," I said, "when I get the chance to start, I'm going to be the best ever." "You and me both," said Todd. "Me and you, Mike, me and you." We looked ahead two, three years. We pictured the Bears in the playoffs, playing in a Super Bowl.

Looking back, all I can say is, thank goodness for real pros like Jim Osborne, Revie Sorey, and Alan Page, who helped me cope with Buddy's digs. They told me to watch how Buddy berated his players but never let anyone else do it, how protective he was of his boys. "But don't ever quit on Buddy," said Osborne. "The one thing he hates is laziness."

4 September, 1981

Dear Teammates:

I am writing this letter to share with you some of my thoughts on the upcoming season. I have never done this in the past but feel compelled to do so this year.

In talking about this year, I think it would be valuable to look back at last year. . . . During the season we were able to make many excuses and point the finger of blame in many directions. It was always the offensive line not working, not throwing the ball to the tight ends, poor coaching offensively, lack of talent defensively, and taking too many gambles on defense. We had the unique ability to find someone to blame for everything. The one thing we never did as a team or as individuals was to accept the responsibility for our own actions and our own play.

At the end of the season, we all felt some changes needed to be made. We are now into the new season. We have been through six weeks of training camp and four preseason games, all of which were rather lackluster. And already we have our built-in excuses: (1) new offensive system; (2) young people in complicated defenses; (3) Hicks waived; (4) Fencik and Jackson out of camp so long; (5) Watts and Earl holding out; (6) Finks; (7) defensive injuries, etc. We have enough finger pointing and excuse making to last a year.

. . . We are not a very good team. At best, we are a .500 team. We lack consistency, we make simple errors. The difference between us and the good teams is that they pay attention to the little things. The only way we are going to improve is if we, as individuals and as a team, take care of the little details and work harder than in the past. We also need to take responsibility for our own actions.

. . . Playing well doesn't just happen. You have to work at it. We can be successful. All we have to do is accept responsibility.

I hope you don't view this letter as just another pep talk. That's not my intent. I think it is a fair and honest assessment of where this team has been and where it can go and what it will take to get there.

Some of you may view this letter as the miscellaneous ramblings of an old football player and you may take what I have said with a grain of salt or not at all, but I would like to offer one last bit of food for thought. I have been part of successful football teams. I have played with great football players, and I know what it takes to have a successful career.

Best of luck to all of us.

Sincerely,

Alan Page

Film and more film. That's all I did, all I cared about. Film. How many times would I—do I—watch the same play? I've lost count, but according to our offensive coordinator, Ed Hughes, who once worked for the indefatigable Dick Vermeil in Philadelphia, the official NFL film-watching record is owned by Vermeil, who once ran a single play back 52 different times. Now, I don't want to brag, but Kim will vouch for the fact that I've exceeded that limit on many, many occasions. She used to watch film with me at home early in the week but gave up after it took me three hours to view the first half of an offense. That's only about 20 or 30 plays, but I watched what every player did on every play, over and over and over again. Today, Kim will occasionally take her chances later in the week, after I've boiled down the film and I'm concentrating on certain individuals or tendencies. But during my early years, I'd take a projector home, set it up downstairs, and run reel after reel, checking different players, assignments, searching for clues to unlock the complexity of the "46," a defense Buddy had dreamed up back in 1978. Just what is the 46? Well, it's actually an 8-2-1 deployment that specializes in creating one-on-one matchups that open up blitz possibilities. The 46 consists of as many as 12 different formations and 80 individual coverages, the real key being our ability to control the opposing offensive tackles with our three down linemen. That's everything. Everything. Because once we control the tackles, it allows us to create confusion and indecision in the offensive line and backfield, giving us a direct route to the quarterback—our ultimate destination.

To Buddy, the beauty of the 46 defense was always set in its simplicity, its flexibility, how easily it could adapt and counteract offensive audibles. In the standard 5-2, 4-3, or 3-4 defense, nine times out of ten the offensive units know exactly where the defensive players will line up and what they'll do. In the 46 you have no idea of this; coverages constantly change. But few clubs can play the 46. It requires intelligence, constant communication, and pure athletic ability. Unfortunately, all three of these were in short supply on the 1981 team. Only Fencik and Hampton were legitimate All-Pros; most of the rest of the club were either veterans hanging on for dear life or young, untested rookies—me included. But every day after practice, Buddy and I would spend two hours reviewing film. Then I'd go home and watch more downstairs until eight or nine at night.

Shortly after Page's letter arrived, we slumped to 1–4 and were sinking fast. Fans were fed up, throwing beer at Neill, who took too much public blame. Most of the guys on the team didn't deserve the chance Neill gave them. I was still watching film, taking guff from Buddy, and hoping to see the light on the 46. "Have patience," said defensive back coach Jim LaRue, the man who quickly became one of my closest friends on the team, a sounding board for ideas, comments, and criticism. He'd been coaching football for more than 30 years, eight as head man at the University of Arizona, where he compiled a winning record, no small feat in the Pac-8 days. A very giving man he was—and still is—willing to answer a question or discuss a play no matter what time of day. We always met on Mondays before the team's 10:00 A.M. film session; he was always wound up, speaking in hurried tones.

"Now Mike, you did a pretty good job out there last week," he'd say in his 78 rpm speech, "but you need to be a little better helping the corner. You were a little late getting there sometimes. I want you to work on technique; you need to get closer to the receiver." "Closer," I said. "I thought I was . . ." LaRue shut me off. "I know, I know," he said. "I'm just telling you. And don't worry so much about the 46. One of these days it's going to click and you're going to have it."

It clicked the week before a Monday night game that year, 1981, against Detroit. I was watching film on Minnesota, which had just edged us 24–21, and Washington, where we'd lost 24–7. By now you could almost hear the laughter around the league. Speaking engagements were a trial; you knew what you would hear: "When are you guys going to draft some football players?" "What's wrong with our team?" or "Why are we playing this crazy 46?" I started taking it personally, leaving right after my speech so as not to get into arguments—or worse. "One day we're going to have the best defense in the league," I said. Folks just laughed.

Buddy never let up on me: Do this. Do that. You're fat. You're slow. You're stupid. You're fat, slow, *and* stupid. I asked what I could do to play. He would just say, "You're a rookie; you can't play."

But that night, down in the basement at home, running the Minnesota game, I suddenly saw something familiar in the guard play. "It's going to be a run," I said aloud, hoping the walls were listening. Sure enough, the Vikes ran. Another play. "Pass to the back," I said. Bingo, a pass to the back. Finally, the book had opened and the words were beginning to make sense.

Monday night, October 19, 1981: Lions 48, Bears 17. I watched the entire game from the sideline, fuming. I can't take it anymore; what more can I do?

I had harassed Buddy, begging to play. I saw who was in there, and if that was the Bears' commitment to excellence, fine, they could have it. I wanted out—a trade, anything. I walked straight into Buddy's office, relishing the fact I was telling this grouchy old sonofagun good-bye.

"Sit down," said Buddy. "Now I'm going to give you the opportunity you've been waiting for. You're going to start this week. But there's one thing I want you to understand. I want you to remember that as long as you have this job you work your butt off. I'm going to be watching you, because I know what you can do. Don't ever lie down on the job. Ever."

Finally, a chance to follow in the footsteps of Bill George and Butkus! I couldn't sleep, watching film almost around the clock, pacing. I called Houston and told my mom and sister to fly up for the game against San Diego.

The first play of the game I looked for the defensive call from the sideline. Now, I've never been afraid to call anything, and Buddy's yelling "Two Z" for a two zone. But Fencik hears "Three Z," a defense that leaves more area to cover. I call time out and trot over. "Are you crazy?!" Buddy screamed. *"No rookie ever calls time out! Get out of here and sit down!"*

So much for my debut. I never played another down. Buddy stayed with the 46 for the rest of the game. But something funny happened: we won, beating the Chargers 20–17 in overtime, holding quarterback Dan Fouts to just 13–43 passing.

I sat through two weeks of Buddy's teasing me in every meeting, morning, noon, and night. Finally he informed me, prior to the Kansas City game, that, yes, I was getting another chance against a good team and a back, Joe Delaney, who was tearing up the league. The first time I hit Delaney, I flowed right through him, a great shot, a Singletary special, and it sucked the air right out of his system. The second time I hit him he went out of the game for good. That was it; I'd found myself. When it was over I had 10 tackles, six solo, recovered a fumble, and was given the game ball. Walking onto the bus after the game, I felt a tap on my leg. It was you-know-who. "I think you did a pretty good job out there today, kid. I think the guys respect you a little now."

I became an even bigger sponge, soaking up the gospel according to Ryan every spare second of the day, picking up game plans on our off-day, Tuesday, memorizing 40–50 pages overnight. I couldn't get enough. I made 72 tackles the last seven games, and the defense stiffened; we held Dallas to 10 points and beat the rugged Oakland Raiders 23–6.

Alan called a team meeting just after the Raiders win. He said despite the victory it appeared Neill would be fired and the coaching staff would go with him. We were practicing at an army base at the time, an icy wind cutting deep into our bones. We knew Alan had tremendous respect and love for Buddy, so we weren't totally surprised when he said, "Why don't we get together and go see Mr. Halas and tell him we want Buddy and the other coaches to stay on?"

George Halas had returned to the Bears in 1980, shortly after his only son, "Mugs," had died of a sudden heart attack. Papa Bear was 85 then and in ill health, but he retained a keen mind when it came to football. I remember one day, after a miserable game, he roared at our offense, *This is a football. Hold on to the *π#%&$ thing!"* This was, after all, a man who had shared the field with Jim Thorpe, who had been MVP of a Rose Bowl, who had played briefly for the Yankees. A man who once, when introduced to President Calvin Coolidge by a U.S. senator—"These gentlemen are the Chicago

Bears"—heard the president say, "How interesting. I've always enjoyed animal acts." Halas was a crusty old pioneer who had breathed life into football when nobody cared about the patient, a man who once roared at a referee, "I don't know what I was talking about, but I'm sure I was right." Old or not, he knew football. Hopefully he would realize how much we needed Buddy. We took a hand vote to decide whether we wanted the coaches to stay. It was unanimous.

"Well," I said, "let's write a letter."

"I'll write it," Alan said, "and we can all sign it."

9 December, 1981

Dear Mr. Halas:

We the undersigned members of the Bears defensive football team are concerned about the future of our team. We recognize that with the disappointing season the Bears have had this year there may be changes in the coaching staff and/or the administration of the team. Our main concern is over the fate of Buddy Ryan and the other defensive coaches.

. . . Buddy has maintained the discipline, morale, pride, and effort we need in order to play well defensively, in spite of the fact that we haven't had much help from our offensive team. It would be easy for us to fold our tent and play out the season, but Buddy and his staff wouldn't let that happen.

Our concern centers on the fact that if Buddy and his staff were replaced, it would set our defensive team back a minimum of two years, and possibly more, by the time we learn a new system and adjust to new coaches.

We feel that if there is to be a change in the coaching staff, Buddy Ryan and his staff should be retained in order to avoid a setback to our defense. We feel we are a good defensive team and that with their help we can be a great defensive team in the near future.

Thank you for considering our request.

Sincerely,

The Chicago Bears Defensive Team

December 22, 1981

Dear Alan:

My thanks to you for sending me the letter asking me to retain Buddy Ryan and his staff and giving me your reasons why.

This is a magnificent letter. It is a beautifully written letter. It is the highest tribute a coach can receive.

I can tell you without fear of contradiction that this is the first time in the 61-year history of the Chicago Bears that such a letter has been written about a Bears coach. I think I can say that this is the first time any owner in the NFL has received such a letter.

I am so fortunate to have you boys on my team.

It was my pleasure meeting with you last Friday, and I am most grateful for your genuine concern for the future of the Chicago Bears. God bless.

Sincerely yours,

Geo. S. Halas

Cameron Park in Waco is a lush, scenic reserve filled with trails and secluded areas frequented by high school sweethearts. It's also become a place where every morning during the 1981 off-season, at about 6:30 or 7:00, Walter Abercrombie, Pittsburgh's number one draft choice, and Dennis Gentry, a Bears draftee (we'd also picked up a quarterback from BYU named McMahon), Cedric Mack of St. Louis, and three or four other pros and I would run and work out. My goals were twofold: consistency and losing weight. I'd played at almost 240 my rookie year, and despite making many all-rookie teams, I wanted to trim down to 225. While I was still at Baylor, my old friend Tom Williams had told me I'd never be a great linebacker until I made up my mind to run, seriously run, and push myself past the obligatory 10-minute mile. So I'd run myself ragged at Baylor covering those running backs one on one. I did the same thing in Cameron Park, always working at cornerback, never at linebacker, practicing my steps, my destination zone drops. Within a month, I could run 45 minutes without stopping.

I also flew to Houston and spent time at Coaches where by now guys like Charlie Joiner of San Diego, Earl Campbell of Houston, Lester Hayes and Cliff Branch of the Raiders, the Redskins' Darryl Green and Vernon Dean were working out. Williams drove us like a mini-Buddy Ryan who, I'm happy to say, had been rehired by George Halas. "I've always been very negative where players are concerned," Williams told me. "I believe if you're a backup player, you perform at a certain level; a starter, another level; All-Conference, another level." I wanted the latter, so we worked hours on end, single coverage against the great All-Pro Joiner and guys like Green who loved to run.

In the afternoon I played racquetball before heading to the movies at night, five or six hours at a pop of watching game film. I watched games I'd played in 1980, charting mistakes, comparing my skills to those of linebacking greats Jack Lambert of Pittsburgh and Randy Gradishar of Denver. I'd watch Todd and Leslie on film, picking up technique. Eight new reels arrived every day, courtesy of the Ryan Express. I'd watch them, send them back, and pick up eight more. This went on almost every day during the spring of 1982. Buddy was always playing amateur psychologist with me, mining whatever mental edge he could, poking, prodding, hoping to strike it rich. He did that spring when he informed me he would no longer "baby" me in practice. "It just can't be like it's been," he said. "You know I've had to protect you out there."

"Baby me? Protect me!"

"Yeah, I know," said Buddy, ignoring the outrage.

"You were kind of wet around the ears, and I had to look after you a little bit. But now I'm going to have to put you out there, and you're going to have to stand on your own."

In the end, I was a lean, mean fighting machine. I had to be. We had hired a new head coach.

"One day, after a particularly miserable game, Halas roared at our offense, 'This is a football. Hold on to the **%¢%¢* thing.'"

5
DITKA

I'll never forget the first day I saw him, this tightly wound spring with the close-set eyes that darted from side to side. Intensity oozed from his skin. The first day, you knew change—for good, for bad, nobody was quite sure—was ahead. He motioned Ted Plumb, our receivers' coach, to call roll. *Roll.* "Well, fellas," Mike Ditka said, calling us together for the first time, "we have only 49 players, and we're going to get out here, and we're going to see who's best. We're going to separate the men from the boys around here, see who wants to work and who doesn't. If you don't want to win, if you don't want to sacrifice, then you don't want to be here."

Even if you did want to "be here," there were times you didn't. He had two minicamps, and one was in Scottsdale, Arizona. It was 90 degrees in the shade, and the training regimen more Green Beret than Bear. Forty-yard dashes until we dropped. Run here. Sprint there. Miles and miles before we slept.

The mumbling and grumbling would have been louder if anyone had enough strength to speak. "I want football players," he said time and time again. "Too many guys around here have too many things going on outside of football."

It boiled down to one word. Pride. Pride in yourself. Pride in your teammates. Pride in your commitment to improve. "I'm proudest of being a Bear," he would say. *Ditka.* It even sounded tough. From the first day, I never doubted his ability to unify and push his team in a positive direction.

His golden rule was that you played by his. He never begged us to do anything. If he said the meeting was at 9:00 A.M., he didn't mean 8:59 or 9:01. You did things a certain way—his way—or you were cut. Yet, at the same time that he was filling the waiver wires, you sensed that he would accept deviation, a free spirit or two. And even though the papers were already calling Halas's hiring him "madness," and knocking Ditka's intelligence, Ditka was going about his business, building a bond between offense and defense that never before existed. "You don't win games with defense," he said. "It takes offense, specialty teams. We're not going to win until *everyone* does his job, because winning and losing depends on all three."

He didn't care whom we played. "They're playing the *Bears!* The *Bears!*" There was nothing phony about him. You'd see him in his office at 5:30 A.M., jogging the halls, then again at midnight, closing the lights. He wanted to be the best. That's all I knew about him. We rarely talked—once or twice a season in depth—but I knew all I needed to know, *wanted* to know. He wanted to be the best. That was good enough for me.

But upon closer inspection, I began to understand his drive. He was the son of a railroad welder from Aliquippa, Pennsylvania, a city not unlike Chicago, a melting pot where you live and learn to rely on your neighbor. Aliquippa is a lunch-bucket town where factory workers find comfort in a warm shower and a shot and a beer after work. Influenced by strong father figures, Ditka grew into an All-American tight end at the University of Pittsburgh, where he played in a white heat, eventually catching more than 400 passes and scoring 43 touchdowns in 12 professional seasons with the Bears, Cowboys, and Eagles. He idolized George Halas, who hired him in 1982 after receiving a personal letter from Ditka, who was applying for Neill's vacant job.

But the transition wasn't easy. He cleaned house for one year. (In a way, he reminded me of a tailor, because whenever someone wasn't putting out or was getting too big for his britches, he'd always be there to cut him down to size. If he sensed a certain swagger seeping into your step, or a head beginning to swell, he always reached for the scissors. Chop, chop. "Hey, just look at it this way," he said. "You could be working for a living. And really, what can you do? I don't think half of you are smart enough to get a job. We don't need you. If you want to leave, get a better deal, fine, leave.") In the strike-shortened season of 1982, we went 3–6, and the press was screaming for Ditka's scalp. McMahon was hot and cold, still learning the offense, and we were still a year away from a blockbuster draft. Halas had died in October 1982, at the age of 88, replaced by current Bears president Mike McCaskey, a Yale graduate, ex–Peace Corps volunteer, Harvard professor, and author of a book on management. Despite having 18 months remaining on a three-year contract, Ditka wasn't sure where he stood with McCaskey, a man with a corporate outlook on life who was in the process of restructuring our front office, paying particular attention to improving our scouting department—we had only two scouts for

50 states, the smallest such department in the league. McCaskey was fully aware that only one pick past the fourth round had ever made our club between 1978 and 1982.

The changes paid off in 1983. Big time talent arrived in the form of Jimbo Covert, Willie Gault, Mike Richardson, Dave Duerson, Pat Dunsmore, Richard Dent, and Mark Bortz. I had made All-Pro my second season, signing a six-year $1.6-million deal with the Bears, much of the money deferred. The contract had been negotiated by Tom Williams, my friend in Houston. "Treat me fair," I said. "I want to die a Bear." My only stipulation: if at any time this contract becomes unfair, we'll work together to bring it up to date.

We finished .500 in 1983. I led the team with 148 tackles and started 16 games, making the Pro Bowl for the first time. We won five of our last six games, including a big 13-3 upset of Super Bowl–bound San Francisco. Willie Gault caught 40 passes; McMahon threw for 2,100 yards despite injury; and Walter Payton ran for his typical 1,400. Even the irascible Ditka was mellowing a bit. After a second straight overtime loss in September, he threw a punch at a metal chest and broke his right hand. Before the next game he jokingly asked us to "win one for Lefty." We did, 31-14, on the road over a tough Denver club. I couldn't wait for the 1985 season to begin.

"Hey, it's not like I negotiated my husband's contract or anything like that . . . but I did ask McCaskey to clear some things up, to define some words as written. It was a neat experience."

—Kim Singletary

6
HOLDING ON AND OUT

WEDNESDAY, DECEMBER 26, 5:00 P.M.

The bus had rumbled along Highway 60, transporting us back to Halas Hall from practice at Morton East High School in Cicero, Illinois. Lost in thought, I'd shaken my head at the sight of a playoff-bound NFL team practicing at a local high school because it seems the club can afford to build an indoor practice facility. As usual, I had been sitting with Todd Bell, my roomie and very close friend. We'd grown extremely close over the last four years, discovering that we shared the same beliefs about women and life. Often we'd talk until 2:00 or 3:00 A.M. on the road, discussing how we yearned to be role models for young people and successful business executives when we left the game. I found Todd to be very different from his on-field image— that of the flamboyant, towel-waving bandit, a style, incidentally, that disturbed many of our teammates. But to know the other Todd is to know the

71

real Todd. The job he did on the field, whether it was filling a hole or running down a tight end—nobody did it better. We thought so much alike, we even wore the same clothes to the airport for road trips. It got to the point where we had to call each other and say, "I'm wearing this today."

On days before games, we always sat talking. During games, we sometimes improvised in the huddle. "You go here," I'd say, "and I'll go there. You take the tight end, I'll cover the back." "I'm going wide, Singletary," he'd say, always chatting. Todd was much more expressive than I with Buddy; he liked to lay his cards on the table. Not that he'd been a teacher's pet; remember, he'd endured three years of "25" and "Taco."

But today, as the bus rumbled along Highway 60, I knew Todd and I were united even in our silence. I'd just been named NFL defensive player of the year; Todd was going to the Pro Bowl as a starter. But we both felt anything but happiness. "Mike, man, I don't know if we're going to see each other anymore," Todd said, "because I'm going to have to get the best deal I can get." He was facing his free agent year. He was making $77,000 at the time. "I know, Todd," I said. "I feel like I should be getting paid like one of the best defensive players in the league."

I came home and talked to Kim. We had been married in May, just seven months earlier, after knowing each other for seven years, since a day at Baylor when she had walked up to my table in the library (I had calculus papers spread all over the place) and asked to sit down. We never really dated in the beginning, preferring to watch television, study, or take walks around campus.

I know it raised some eyebrows when Kim and I started seriously seeing each other. But honestly, I never consciously set out to date a certain color or culture of woman. Actually, I doubted I'd ever find the "right" woman, at least for me, since I'd set up a long list of ground rules that any prospective date had to pass before I'd even consider asking her out. She couldn't drink. Or smoke. Or wear short dresses. She couldn't do drugs. Guys on the team thought I was crazy, from another time period, and maybe I was. But that's the type of woman I was after—old-fashioned, strong, committed to helping her husband be the best he could be—no matter what profession he chose.

In short, she had to be willing to make some sacrifices—just as I was—to build a better future. Kim was all of that. She'd been raised in a Christian home and proved to be pretty patriotic herself. She rallied around me when the going got tough; she didn't head for the front door at the first sign of sacrifice like so many women—and men—today; she wasn't like those wives who complain that if their husband "doesn't buy me a new house this winter or get me some new jewelery, me and the baby are going to be up and gone." What type of marriage do you have if it's based solely on materialistic pleasures? A happiness that is measured in dollars and cents?

Before I asked Kim to marry me in 1983, I was torn by such questions. I almost stayed single and went into the ministry. Instead I sat down with Kim, talked about hopes, dreams, remembering what Tom Williams had once told me: "Son," he said, "a lot of people get married but they don't realize marriage doesn't have anything to do with weddings and ceremony. It's what happens after the wedding. The trials. The tribulations. The tough times. Son, never get married until you're sure you can't live without that other person."

In the end, that's how I felt. Making all pro, winning the Super Bowl, wouldn't mean nearly as much without Kim there to share it with me. I wanted her by my side. Today Kim is everything I need—a good, strong, faithful woman, giving, understanding, willing to give of herself without demanding immediate "balance" in return. Maybe she was old-fashioned in her support of my goals. I don't know. I do know she added and still adds another dimension to my life, her spontaneous, freewheeling spirit, a sharp and welcome contrast to my cautious nature. I always said before getting married I'd want my daughter to mirror my wife. I think a daughter like Kim would be easy to understand and a blessing from above.

"Sweetheart," I said, "I think I'm going to have to go ahead and do what I have to do. I don't know how tough it's going to get, but I don't think it's going to be a problem."

I couldn't have been more wrong. The next day, watching film of the Redskins, I couldn't get the contract off my mind. Normally, I'm a guy who doesn't believe in going against the system, as long as I sign my name on something with full understanding of the consequences. But when I signed my contract in 1983, I was under the oral impression that if the existing contract became unfair at any time, general manager Jerry Vainisi would work something out. Well, in 1984 the Bears signed Wilber, who was in a bidding war with a USFL team, for $1.6 million for four years, much of it deferred. Wilber had been a college superstar at Florida, the words "tackle by Wilber Marshall" a very long-playing record. His junior and senior years Wilber accounted for 218 tackles and 12 sacks. But Buddy was rough on him right from the start, calling him "stupid"—despite the fact Wilber was an academic All-American in school—and Wilber couldn't adjust. He was the last one to show for practice, the first one out the door at night. He didn't even stop to shower sometimes. Al Harris was starting, and Wilber made only 19 tackles in 15 games, unwilling to prove to Buddy he wanted to play. And that's the one thing about Mr. Ryan. He never begs.

I wasn't jealous or bitter over Wilber's deal. Anytime a player can raise the living standard in the NFL, I'm all for it. Wilber wasn't my argument. I wanted *real* dollars. No annuities. It was as simple as that. Still, I told Wilber I could relate to his dilemma; after all, I'd sat behind Kunz my first year. But at the same time, I told him, "Wilber, how do you expect to start if you're sitting on the sidelines, hurt all the time? Buddy will never put you in there unless you show him something." I truly like him. But I felt the same way about the Bears. They had to show me something. I went to Vainisi and said, "I can't play this game unless something is done with my contract." "We'll get something done, Mike, don't worry," Jerry answered. "Just go ahead and study; do what you have to do." I met him on the Friday night before the 'Skins game. "Jerry, where do you think I am as far as defensive players in the league go?" I asked. "Mike, no doubt in my mind, you're one of the best," he said. "Well," I said, "why can't I be paid like one of the best?"

Vainisi went on about contract obligations, then he asked me to rate myself. I said, "I'm definitely in the top three—in a class with Lawrence Taylor, (now with the New York Giants) and Hugh Green of Tampa Bay." "I don't know," Vainisi said. "Listen," I said, "you know what you've got. Someone who comes in early every morning, who gives you everything he's got. I'm there before the coaches, and when I leave nobody is around except me and Coach Ditka. I think I deserve to be treated fairly, and in my mind that's in the top two or three."

Vainisi told me it would take time. Well, our win over Washington came and went. So did a 23–0 embarrassment to San Francisco in the NFC championship game, a loss that eventually taught this team how to win. I remember being down near one end zone that day, the seconds ticking away, and looking up at a crowd gone mad. "We'll be back, we'll be back," I screamed. On the flight home, that's all we talked about. *"We'll be back!"* I sat across the aisle from McMahon and we consoled each other. "You guys really played your asses off," he said. "We just couldn't get a damn thing going." Jimbo Covert stuck his head in. "We're going to do it, Mike. We gotta do it. It'll give us something to hang on to for next year."

During the off-season, every time I called Vainisi he was busy or out—a scouting combine meeting to attend, a draft decision to make. He sent me a "new" contract, but it was nothing more than a rehash—swapping some cash now for an annuity program later. It was still six years. It was still the same money. I took one look and threw the papers in the trash.

"This is not what I'm talking about," I told him.

"Mike, we don't renegotiate," he said. "It's a club policy."

"Why didn't you tell me that when I signed my last contract?"

I told him not to expect me at minicamp in May. I could sense they didn't believe me—Samurai would never miss a minicamp—but I felt betrayed. I'm old-fashioned, a believer in the team, and I refuse to go out and give 150 percent if my heart's not in it. I'm not a Bear just when I'm playing; it's part of my life, my blood. The Bears were about to see the stubborn side of my heritage.

WEDNESDAY, MAY 15, 1985, 8:30 A.M.

Workout time with Danny Rains. Danny's a great friend, a brother to me. We met four years ago when he was signed as a linebacker in May 1982 by the

Bears, a tough, relentless athlete the club had
picked out of a minor league football film when
they were looking at another player. We'd both
come from large families, so we shared the bonds
and burdens of having so many brothers and sisters
and a belief in God. He had spent much of 1982–83
on the reserve list recuperating from elbow and leg
injuries; the last two seasons he'd developed into a
very valued special teams player. He loves to work,
so we killed each other in workouts, following a
tight schedule almost every morning. Light breakfast, then a ride over to the Hill. Not just any hill, but
a boat ramp near Lake Forest worthy of a World
Cup slalom competition. We'd run 20, 30, 40, sometimes 50 of those hills. Always the same routine:
sprint up, walk down. Sometimes we'd sprint up
backwards, working on our pass drops. I even tried
it with a 30-pound vest (not for long, though). And
occasionally other players would drop by—defensive back Shaun Gayle, tight end Pat Dunsmore,
Fencik, tight end Tim Wrightman, Gentry, and Leslie Frazier, but they'd run 10 or so and leave.

In June I left Chicago for Houston to train with
Tom Williams. Again I covered Joiner and others,
always playing corner. People ask how I can play
the pass so well. The hill, dedication, and coaches like
Tom Williams, that's how. By now, Halas Hall was a
memory; I hadn't set foot inside the building since
our loss to San Francisco. Then Vainisi called. I told
him I wasn't coming to minicamp. "We'll get things
straight," he said. "You have no intention of getting
things straight," I answered. "I'm tired of talking
about it. I don't know who you think I am. I was
willing to die for the Bears. But before I go out and
play the type of football I'm capable of playing, you
have to show me this organization is as loyal to me
as I am to it. And right now, I don't feel that. I feel
betrayed."

DAY BEFORE MINICAMP, MAY 22

Vainisi called again. Said the Bears were standing firm. There would be no renegotiation. "Don't tell me you don't renegotiate," I said. "If you're not going to pay me, then trade me."

"No, we're not going to do that," Jerry said.

Fine. I didn't want to do it, but I knew I had the tools, the business talent, to walk away. We didn't need much money. We could sell the house, move to Dallas, and you could be reading about me in some business magazine in a couple of years. Still, it didn't help that, by now, the news media in Chicago were all over the holdout. Generally, I respect all writers who cover the Bears—Don Pierson, Ed Sherman, Bob Verdi, Bernie Lincicome at the *Tribune*, Kevin Lamb, Brian Hewitt, Dan Pompei, Ray Sons, Ron Rapoport with the *Sun-Times*, Randy Minkoff of UPI, suburban writers like Terry Bannon of the *Herald*. They work hard at developing fresh stories every day. They're also very straightforward, anything but mouthpieces for the Bears organization. But it was tough to read articles intimating that I was greedy and uncaring about my teammates.

But at least I wasn't alone. A source of strength during this trying time was something we called the Four Corners. Todd, Al, Richard Dent, and I were the corners, all holding out, holding on, determined not to break. Todd wanted more than the $1.6 million over four years the Bears were offering; Al refused a three-year, $825,000 deal; and Richard, who had led the NFL in sacks in 1984, was petrified at the prospect of playing for $90,000 in 1985. All through the summer we talked almost every day, ministering to each other. I never stopped working out, watching film at home, hoping something would happen.

July 15

Training camp opened today. Memories of Platteville, population 5,751, in extreme southwest Wisconsin, along the Little Platte River, came flooding back. Memories of this tiny trade center for farming, dairying, lead and zinc mining; of the crop dusters sitting idle at airports; of Hampton and McMichael singing "Up Against the Wall Redneck Mother," at one local function; of Anthony Hutchinson, a running back released by the club in 1984, beating the pants off Otis, L.A., and Leslie on the pool table; of receivers coach Plumb bustling into two-a-days with the zeal of a missionary, chirping away—"Boys, it's great to be alive. What a great day to work"—oblivious to our miseries; of McMahon pulling into camp in a limo and shades, beer in hand. Terribly, like the cows in pastoral Platteville, I could feel my career being put out to pasture.

At times like this, I turned to the Bible and the book of Job, for there's not a character you'll respect more, a man the Lord allowed fate to take, to use, knowing Job wouldn't lose faith. As the story goes, Job is a prosperous man in the East whose seven sons and daughters were killed by Satan, but he never lost faith. Finally, God not only returned what was Job's but doubled his riches in reward for his faith. At other times I'd turn to the words of the apostle Peter—how focused he was, so solid in his beliefs. I tied myself to the Lord, not trusting my eyes or the club's words, knowing in my heart that money wasn't the answer, it wasn't going to bring me back. It was the principle. Kim and I prayed at breakfast, lunch, and dinner. "Give me a sign," I said. "I've come to a crossroad; maybe it's time to give it up."

"Are you serious?" Kim said one day. "I've never seen you this way."

"Yes," I said. "I'm very serious."

By now, the Bears were already two games into the exhibition season. Late one night Kim and I were lying in bed, lost in thought. "It means a lot of things are going to have to go," I said. "We may not have a nice car, fine clothes. You may be looking for the last time at a nice house of your own. Maybe I have to go out there and be an evangelist. It doesn't mean we have to be poor if we walk with the Lord, but it does mean sacrifice."

"It doesn't matter," Kim said. "I knew when we got married that we'd go through things unlike anyone else, because you're how you are. So whatever you say in this is fine with me. I'm with you."

SUNDAY, JULY 27, 1985, 8:30 A.M.

Richard called today. "I think I'm going in," he said. I can tell he's confused. Richard was drafted in the eighth round out of Tennessee State, the school that produced dominating defensive ends like Too Tall Jones, Claude Humphrey, and Cleveland Elam. And Richard's as quick with the ladies as he is off the ball. "Oh, you're looking lovely," he'll say, all the while flashing those bedroom eyes. Away from the game he likes to ride horses, swim, play racquetball. Music was his life growing up, the third of nine children, the son of an Atlanta printer and a mother who owned her own catering service. Richard has made $60,000 and $70,000 the last two years; and the thought of playing for $90,000 this year, 10 percent of what he could make in an open market— if the NFL had the open market—is killing him. But he wants to play.

"If that's what you want to do, go ahead," I said.

He waited one more week, until August 4. The club evidently came across with some insurance policy. "Mike," Richard explained on the phone,

"I'm going to go." "Good luck to you, Richard," I said. "Don't feel like you're letting us down. You have to do what you have to do. Whether you're right or wrong, only time will tell." The Four Corners had suddenly become the Three Musketeers. But honestly I felt alone, isolated from Todd and Al, who were both free agents. I had a contract; I could report anytime.

Vainisi was out of my negotiations by now, replaced first by Ed McCaskey, chairman of the board of the Bears, and finally by the club president himself, Mike McCaskey. No matter who sat on the other side of the table, it wasn't working. We decided to put the house up for sale, move to Houston, and pursue business opportunities. I also intended to stay in shape. I was reading Proverbs a lot, a book that talks about a man and his pride. Was pride standing in my way? Sometimes a man's pride is more powerful than alcohol or drugs, forcing him into dangerous situations, separating himself from reason.

Mike McCaskey is a new-breed owner who favors blue shirts, red ties, and an uncluttered desk. His piercing blue eyes contrast nicely with distinguished gray hair and expensive suits. He is a man who enjoys using words like *finite* and *continuum.* And the sound of his own voice.

"It was a very tough negotiation," said McCaskey. "We both took our points of view very seriously. Neither of us was going to back down. The point we always make with the players is, the Bears cannot afford to lose money. The team is the only asset our family has, and we expect to own the team into the 1990s and beyond. It's a fact of life that the Bears cannot reach into other pockets. We have to take a finite pile of resources and be fair in meeting our obligations."

"Fine," I said, when I first heard that opening argument. "But I'm not playing for what I'm making." McCaskey would listen, then lecture on, describing club problems, diminishing returns. I'd just point to my list and say: "No. 2, I want the contract reduced to four years." Or I would compare my salary to those of fellow linebackers Lance Mehl of the Jets, Tom Cousineau of Cleveland, Carl Banks in New York, all making more money than I was and none, as far as I knew, defensive MVPs of any league. "I'm better than any of those guys," I said. "I turn on the lights in the morning and turn them off at night."

At this point, voices usually went up, gesturing began. One time, the words got a little hot, and McCaskey began gesturing violently until, out of the corner of his eye, he noticed a reporter watching our battle through the picture window in McCaskey's office, which overlooks our Halas Hall practice field. The reporter was making a beeline for the window. McCaskey quickly shut the drapes. Then he said: "Other teams have millions more money, Michael. We're trying to field a team."

"But we had an understanding . . ."

McCaskey: "I had serious doubts about any verbal agreement. It was nobody's fault in particular. Vainisi made it clear to me he made no promises, even if there was terrific improvement. I'm guessing Mike's agent made the job of selling the contract easier by saying something like, 'You know, the Bears will renegotiate if you do this or that.'"

SATURDAY, AUGUST 10, 1985, 3:00 P.M.

I saw Danny after practice today. He and Debbie are staying with us until they find an apartment, so Danny's doing double duty, acting as a messenger, passing along information between Buddy and me.

"Just tell him I'm working my butt off, harder than anyone over there, and I guarantee I'll be ready to play when I come in," I said. "Buddy already knows that; don't worry," Danny said. "He says he misses you but knows it's something you've got to do."

MONDAY, AUGUST 19, 1985, 1:30 P.M.

I'll never forget this day. Round two was a three-hour slugfest with McCaskey. I've had it with his bottom-line football, business-as-usual mentality, his stockholder responsibilities. Finally, I couldn't control myself. "Have you ever played football?" I screamed. It startled him. But he composed himself, saying, "Why, yes, I played when I was in college, at Yale. I was a wide receiver." "Wide receiver!" My tone was mocking. "What do they know?"

Enough, it appeared, to end a conversation. "Well, Mike," he said, "It looks like you're not going to be a Bear." I left his office in silent rage.

McCaskey: "It came to a point where what his principles demanded of him and what my responsibilities demanded of me meant he would not be in a Chicago Bear uniform. I was tremendously depressed. I know how important he is to the team, his leadership, his work habits. I stared out my window for a long time after he left, wondering what it all might mean."

AUGUST 19, 1985, 3:00 P.M.

Time to pack, to make last-minute phone calls and head for Houston. The Bears have turned on me. It didn't matter if I played or was released; I was going to follow the Lord, to trust Him. I remember the players who called or stopped by—Walter, Matt Suhey, Jimbo. "Is there anything we can do?" Walter said. "We need you, Mike," added Suhey. "Don't get to the point where you're forced to make a decision."

I had told them money wasn't a factor, and it wasn't. Money can be taken from a person. I felt, if I ran back to camp, I couldn't look them in the face and say I'm a leader. I would have been there because I was afraid my family would be on the street, that I was going to have to hustle in life outside football. I couldn't do that.

MONDAY, AUGUST 19, 1985, 8:00 P.M.

I was walking outside our suburban home, staring at the moon when the thought hit me, a blindsided emotion I never expected: Call Mike McCaskey. Set another meeting. I shook my head; we'd just talked; it was over. But then I called. "Let's meet tomorrow," I said.

"What time?" said McCaskey.

TUESDAY, AUGUST 20, 1985, 3:30 P.M.

Two-thirds of the contract is complete. We saw eye to eye for the first time today, thanks in large part to a new member of the negotiating team—Kim Singletary. I had brought a copy of the contract home, and she questioned some of the wording. The next day, she sat quietly in McCaskey's office, speaking only when she sensed tension rising. Subtly, she'd ask questions, promote a possibility, using words that often led to agreement. McCaskey agreed to reduce my contract to four years. "You were the only Bear with a six-year deal, so I feel that's fair," he said. Oh, there's still confusion over how certain incentives will be paid but we're making progress. Bears offered a package that at best—if we went to the Super Bowl and I won league MVP—could more than double my base salary. But McCaskey wanted to deduct $50,000 of my incentive money as a penalty; in effect, a warning to other Bears not to barge into his office every time they felt underpaid.

I understood his rationale and accepted it, believing that the money would be returned in 1986, providing I had a better season. I also understood the incentive money would double. Kim straightened that out; the $50,000 was forfeited; the Bears package contained no provisions for double compensation. Still, it was fair; I would be paid based on my play. That's all I ever wanted.

WEDNESDAY, AUGUST 21, 1985

Should have practiced this morning, five days before our Dallas exhibition game, but the contract was not signed. We had a handshake deal, but I want everything on paper—no more surprises. We spent the entire morning arguing over one last detail, my right to renegotiate future contracts on the basis of superior performance. Word was already buzzing around camp that I'd signed, leaving Ditka upset over my absence at morning practice.

"Where's Singletary? Where's Singletary?" reporters kept asking. "I don't know," Ditka snapped. "Don't ask me."

When the deal was done, I rushed to his office. On his desk sits a big sign. "Communicate," it says. And I've always believed one of Ditka's biggest assets as a coach is his uncanny ability to find the "hot" button on every player and know exactly when to push it. With Walter, for example, he never downgrades him directly, always saying things like, "Pick it up a little, son" or "Run it on in there." To McMahon he says anything, knowing Jim is going to respond to almost any stimulus. Me, well, I figure I'm rowing in the same boat as McMahon.

"Damn," Ditka said as soon as I walked in. "I can't

understand what's going on. You were supposed to be at practice, and you didn't come out. You're not playing this week."

"Why the hell can't I play? I'm ready. I'm as ready as any guy out there," I countered.

"It's not the same, and I'm telling you you're not going to play."

Now I was fired up. He'd hit my hot button all right—playing. "The hell I'm not going to play. I'm gonna play. And I'm gonna start."

Ditka wouldn't budge. "You're not ready; there's no way you can be ready."

"Listen," I said. "I had to get something straight on paper up there. There's no way in the world I'm going to go out there on the field when I have something else on my mind. If that had been you, you would have done the same thing. What would you rather I do? Come out there and practice this morning and not take care of business? Next week I'm in the same boat. No way. I wanted to get it straight before I ever hit the field. That way it's out of sight and out of mind."

With that, I quickly got out of sight before Ditka went out of his mind.

McCaskey walked me down to the weight room where the team was working out after afternoon practice. "Gentlemen," he said, "I'd like to introduce you to our newest team member, Mike Singletary." Otis came up and gave me—what else?—a giant Bear hug. "Samurai, you back, man? You back?" "Yeah, I'm back." Otis said, "Oh, all right, we're ready to go now, ready to go." Leslie and Wilber joined in, as did most of the rest of the guys. Otis was especially glad to have the boys back together again.

At 6'4", 235 pounds, Otis Wilson fits the image of a fiery, flamboyant football player, one who sometimes, I think, wants to be remembered more as an international lover than as an All-Pro linebacker. We have a strange relationship; we're night and day in our approach to life, but I love Otis like a brother. I worry about him more than any player on the club. I question, sometimes, his ideas on life, believing Otis figures sometimes that he came into pro ball with almost nothing, and if he leaves with about the same, he hasn't lost anything. His cocky attitude and buoyant personality—"I'll stop talking when they lay me in a box and throw the dirt down"—is a cover, perhaps, for a certain emptiness that has settled into his soul. Otis grew up on the mean streets of the Brownsville section of Brooklyn and dominated play all through high school and college, at Louisville. Early on with the Bears he suggested that we get together. "You and I never do anything on our days off," he told me one day in 1983. So off we went to lunch and a movie, *Scarface*. But for some reason, I felt uncomfortable, a constant need to call Kim. When I got home, tears were running down my cheeks.

"What's the matter?" said Kim, seeing my tears. "Do you want to break up?"

"Otis." It was all I could say.

Then I spoke. "I have this bad feeling something's going to happen to him. I don't know, maybe it was the violence in the movie. I actually looked under our car before we left. He couldn't sit still, always making calls. I don't want anything to happen to him." Nothing has ever happened to him, and I love Otis more today than ever, maybe because he reminds me so much of Grady, on the edge, searching. I just hope he finds what he's searching for.

THURSDAY, AUGUST 22, 1985

First full day back. I sense the club is motivated but unsettled, tiptoeing along, searching for its own identity. The only real spirit in camp are the ghosts of Todd and Al Harris, which seem to hover over every practice and work their way into every conversation. We're 1–2 in preseason awaiting Dallas, with Wilber and strong safety Dave Duerson fighting battles of insecurity. Hampton's knee is killing him; Fencik is slowly recovering from a groin injury. Still, Buddy's in rare form. He greeted me today with up-downs, then an interception drill, where he threw every ball so far over my head that I couldn't touch it without a small plane. "Ha, ha," Buddy laughed, throwing another air ball. "You're out of shape, Samurai. You're too short to get that ball. C'mon, jump for it!" My penalty: more grass drills. I don't care. I'm happy to be a Bear again.

After practice, I outlined my goals for the 1985 season to Buddy: win the Super Bowl and win the league MVP award. I would be the first defensive player to win that honor since Alan Page in 1971.

"Gee, I don't know, Samurai," Buddy said. "You don't get to make all the glamour plays, the interceptions, the sacks . . . you're really going to have to specialize in what you do, make people recognize you. And you have to work like nobody's business.

"Buddy, what are my chances? On a scale of 1 to 10."

He looked me straight in the eye. "Ten," he said. "No chance."

"I can't believe that."

"Sorry, but that's just the way it is."

10:00 P.M.

It only took one day to see Buddy is pushing the 46 harder than ever this year, refining it, simplifying it, keying it to the new personnel. I've always said that the greatness in Buddy Ryan lies in his ability to

simplify. It took him a while to understand what
makes each of us tick. But now, after a 90-minute
chalk talk on Wednesday morning, and the subse-
quent concentration drills (where we slowly walk
through each defensive option), it's impossible for
us to miss an assignment. Plus, Buddy never says,
"Make sure you go 10 yards and watch for the *X*
guy." Instead, he just says, "Look, all you have to do
is stay underneath the guy on combo one." He
makes the system fit the players and the plays.
That's the beauty of Buddy: he's willing to change,
his ego willing to listen when common sense tells
him to adjust. For example, in 1983 and early '84,
teams would use three tight ends on a play, and
we'd still have two safeties in the game. One day
Buddy said, "Samurai, they're going to run the ball.
Why don't we just go with two cornerbacks and a
weak safety? I'm going to send more linebackers in
there." Other times, a team would try to shake us
up, sending men in motion, shifting, switching. The
bottom line with Buddy always was "Does it mean
anything to us?" In time, I began to see the game
through his eyes, to notice how a quarterback will
look in one direction when throwing to the tight
end, another on a screen. And if you missed a call, at
least during film sessions Buddy never made you
feel stupid, and his game plan always made sense.

   Great athletes have always been the key to the
success of the 46, and this year even more so. You
needed people like Hampton, McMichael, Hartenstine, and this rookie, Perry, up front. Nobody can
block Hampton one on one for long; McMichael's a
load, and Hartenstine plays the run as well as
anyone in the game. On the end, Dent lives for
getting upfield, and outside Wilber has great speed
and cover ability, while Otis is an intimidator. Fencik? When he isn't worried about getting another

groin injury and plays to his potential, he hits as hard as any safety in the league.

Because of this experience and athletic talent, Buddy had come up with something you could call the Buddy System, AFC in our book—Automatic Front Coverage. Boiled down, it's an audiblized defensive system in which I call coverages on the basis of formations and tendencies I pick up as the team breaks the huddle and comes to the line of scrimmage. If they adjust, I adjust. If they audible, so do I. In effect, we play a chess game in cleats controlled by a 30-second time clock.

I can't tell you how many times when I was coming off the field during a game Buddy has said, "I want to see how they're blocking the 46. Run Red 17–7—or Blue Cover 1 or White Single 46." After the first series, we always report back to Buddy:

"Richard, did the running back pick you up?"

"Yeah, he picked me up."

"Hampton, how they blocking you?"

"Double team."

"Mike, how about you?"

"The other back took me."

"Look, OK, then let's run an outside blitz."

And we ran it and ran it until the well ran dry. Oh, we don't make it obvious, telegraphing our intentions, but once Buddy smells blood, he'll blitz every down. It doesn't make any difference to him. He doesn't care what the next guy is saying. He goes with what he feels. And sooner or later, the quarterback is going to feel it, too.

I told Tom Williams my goal of becoming MVP. He tried to talk me out of it. "It's always a running back or a quarterback," he said. "But if that's what you want, if you want to be the best, you're going to have to play like the best." I asked him to critique my performance each week, to expect a Monday morning phone call. I told him I was intent on being the best, ranking with Willie Lanier, who played for Kansas City, Ray Nitschke of Green Bay, and Dick Butkus as a middle linebacker. Yet I wanted to cover wide outs and tight ends like Willie Brown, the former Oakland Raider All-Pro. With Lanier and Butkus, you could feel their intensity through the TV screen; I was awed by their teeth-rattling hits, their sixth sense when it came to being around the football. The Best. That's what I wanted to be.

As you can tell, I'm rather compulsive about my ranking in the game. I badger Tom, Buddy, even Ditka with the same three questions: "Where am I? How am I doing? Where do I rate?" Sometimes Buddy just blows his stack. "Just keep doing what you're doing!" he says, "I don't see what you're doing wrong. You're running well, playing the pass; you're doing everything you have to do. Why do you keep askin' me?"

Why do I? Most anyone would be satisfied with my accomplishments, but to me it's not being a leader, winning awards, breaking helmets. I want to be able to look at a game film one day and see no mistakes, everything 100-percent perfect. Sometimes, late at night, downstairs or over at Halas Hall, I see a mistake—a miscall, an overreaction—and I'm upset because I want to be known, to be remembered, as an athlete without weakness, someone who opposing coaches know is going to out-think, out-hit, and out-anything, whatever it takes to win.

I guess, ultimately, I'm striving to make the Singletary name something special, just as every man on this team is trying to do for Chicago and the Bears. I look at my family, the superficiality, the fairy-tale nightmare, my diverse heritage, and I want to grow up to be the best American I can be. That's why I buy only American cars, American clothes. I'm forming a foundation by doing my part to build a better America, a world family, because, after all, aren't we all part of one family, His family? Therefore, in my mind, I'm not part of a minority but a majority. I want perfection because I'm playing for the glory of God. Yet at the same time, I want to show the world the brilliance of Buddy Ryan. Moreover, I believe someday I will own a multimillion-dollar corporation, and when my employees look me in the eye, I want them to know we're both part of something special. My father started as a minister, and he got lost along the way. My mother, and there's no better person, suffered through a painful marriage. It affected all her children. I've got nieces now who are pregnant and unmarried, and it makes me angry. Why can't they understand how important family is, the importance of working hard, reaching for the highest mountain? Personally, I'm the type of guy who won't take no for an answer when it comes to getting a job. I'd just say, "I can take on any guy you got here, and I'm going to be here before he gets here, and I'll be here when he leaves. Do I get the job or not? Call the cops and tell them to come and get me because I'm not leaving."

The same philosophy comes across on the field, only in a much more violent manner. That's the way, I hope, as this season progresses, the Chicago Bears will play football. I sense this team can live with the contract disputes, the holdouts, this unwavering swell of uninterrupted adversity. Pre-Ditka, the team's soul vanished, replaced by bickering and backstabbing. But, somehow, this is a different Bears team, the schism between offense and defense repaired. We know we have 23 games to play if we're to accomplish our goals, and there's no time for cheap shots or cheaper talk. Ditka made that all quite clear today when he addressed the entire team. "You don't win games with defense," he said. "You don't win them with offense. Or special teams. You win or lose because of one thing. T-E-A-M. Team."

I know we can do it. But right now, I'm not completely sure how.

"Fridge, the poor guy, has taken endless abuse since Day One, mostly from Hampton who's always telling him, 'Biscuit, you look hungry,' calling him 'Mudslide' or worse."

"You can't give them a Knute Rockne speech every week. I tried to create a crisis. I thought they could relate and understand. The main thing was I always tried to put us in a role of the underdog, the outcast, the team that nobody liked. I know that wasn't true. But this was one of the ways I had to deal with them." —Mike Ditka

7
SEPTEMBER 1985

The weather pattern in Chicago this time of year is so unpredictable. Cold one day, Indian summer the next. The Bears seem to be experiencing the same phenomenon. I feel we're ready for the season, but uncertain about the days ahead.

A lot of folks are saying it's a good thing we were playing Tampa Bay our first game. Those folks must be sitting in the stands, because Tampa Bay, while it doesn't get a great deal of public respect, is really one of the best teams in the NFL. I can't figure out why the Bucs don't win more. They have a great tight end, the best in the business in Jimmy Giles and, for my money, the best all-around back in the league, James Wilder, as well as a dependable quarterback in Steve DeBerg. Not only is Wilder strong and fast, but he plays with a heart the size of Halas Hall. The man never gives up.

McMahon's hurting, but that doesn't stop him from predicting it will take 28 to 31 points to win. He knows our defense is struggling. He's right, but that doesn't preclude me from taking my weekly run over to the record shop after practice on Saturday. Around 11:30 A.M. I drove over to Big Apple Records near the house, searching out my music for the week. With music, I can control or express my emotions. I own more than 200 tapes and records, everything from Luther Vandross to Bach, to rock, to soul. Isaac Hayes is one of my favorite artists for the way his songs speak to life. My musical tastes, however, are ever changing, evolving, subject to the team we play, the mood I'm in. For a physical team like Tampa Bay or Green Bay, I lean more toward high-energy sound—rock or hard jazz. For hard-hitting games, I love to listen to Tina Turner's "I Might Have Been Queen" from her *Private Dancer* album. Two particular stanzas from that song have always hit close to home:

> I'm a new pair of eyes
> An original mind
> With my senses of old
> And the heart of a giant
> And I'm searching through the wreckage
> For some recollection
> That I might have been queen.
>
> I look up to the stars
> With my perfect memory
> I look through it all
> And my future's no shock to me
> I look down but I see no tragedy
> I look up to my past
> A spirit running free
> I look down and I'm there in history
> I'm a soul survivor . . .

For a more cerebral game, say against Miami or San Francisco, I try to dial down, to ease my anger with Bach or Billy Joel. Sometimes Kim will try to anticipate a mood. "You've got that Kenny Rogers tape," she'll say. "But I don't want Kenny Rogers," I say. "I want Dionne Warwick." Picky, picky.

SATURDAY, SEPTEMBER 7, McCORMICK CENTER HOTEL, SOUTH SIDE CHICAGO, 10:00 P.M.

At the defensive meeting tonight, Buddy gave us one of his standard country-cousin speeches, the game plan rolled up in the right hand, tapping his left. He's cooked up a couple of new specials for the Bucs; one has Otis moving into one of the center gaps next to the rookie, William Perry. Buddy called it "5-2 Alan" after Page. "Now we've got a pretty good game plan here," he told us. "Now you people just have to go out and execute it. Doesn't mean a damn thing if you don't. Now let's go out there tomorrow and do it."

Hardly Winston Churchill or FDR fireside in the White House, but to us it meant one thing: Buddy was ready. Play it the way it's planned and you'll win. Mess up and chances are you'll lose. The plans are always that good. So is the philosophy: Don't sit back taking punches; throw them. Blitz, mix coverage, force the Bucs into a defensive offensive position.

I've crawled into bed at the McCormick, slipped on my headphones, and, once again, for a final time, glanced through my playbook. My habits during this period on the eve of a game rarely vary: I listen to music, read the Bible, talk to Kim, and then go to bed. Sometimes I read a lot of Scripture, other times only a verse or two. It depends on my mood. The only true constant on game night is Kim calling to ask how I feel—"Pretty good," I said early tonight, "but I have to watch a little bit more film"— and a mental exercise I call visualization, whereby I play an imaginary game over and over in my head, anticipating situations, calls, audibles, formations that I've run hundreds of times on the screen. I have to know everything—*everything*—that can possibly happen. If not, I can't sleep.

In the morning, I'll have breakfast, tune into either Jimmy Swaggart or Robert Schuller, my favorite TV evangelists, before heading off to the locker room, where slowly but surely I'll change into a very different person. My voice will change, growing louder as I near the field. I'll scream. The metamorphosis has always been something of a mystery to fans: How could a quiet, mild-mannered person pillage and plunder on the field? I don't have any single answer, only the knowledge that when I step onto the field I'm playing for the glory of God and I won't settle for second best. I won't leave one ounce of energy in the locker room. It's funny, Christianity is one of the things I really won't debate. Even when I see things I think aren't Christian, it doesn't give me the right to judge, because, at times, I've done things I have no business doing. So, unless a person is really off-base, I won't discuss it because there are many interpretations of the Christian life, and I'm living my life in the way I know I can answer to the Lord. Still, God gave me the ability to play, and my gift to him is what I do with it. I feel that, if I loll around and don't give 100 percent, He'll take it away.

My bottom-line philosophy, I guess, is whatever you have, take it, multiply it as much as you can, and then give, whether it's on the field, the office, or at home. I thank God that He really knows my heart. He knows what I intend to do, and it doesn't matter what Joe Blow thinks about my Christianity or my life. When I'm out on the field, I want the other player to know I'm not going to hurt him; I want him to pay me as much respect as I'm paying him.

Unfortunately, we left our game in the locker room the first half. With Wilder running, well, wild, the Bucs led 28–17. Nobody was thinking; everyone was leaning on the blocks. Ditka didn't say a word. Buddy wasn't so kind. "I just want to let you guys know you were pitiful out there. I'm not blowing smoke up your butt; you were terrible."

The tide finally turned on an interception by Leslie (a quiet, uncomplaining man who's grown into one of my closest friends on the team). Dent tipped DeBerg's throw on the second play of the second half, and Leslie returned it 29 yards. It lit a fire under McMahon, who went on to complete a club record 23 passes, sparking a 38–28 victory. I could feel the holdout hurt me today; I was out of step almost all day, but one time, in the first half, it finally came together. The down, distance, the extra film work. We were in our third-down nickel defense, and I was lined up over the tight end Jimmie Giles. Wilder was split off to the weak side. I remembered the formation from watching pre-season film on the Bucs. So when Giles didn't fire out—unusual in a third-down pass situation—I screamed, "Draw, draw, draw," pointing to a hole over center. Sure enough, DeBerg couldn't audible in time, Wilder went for the hole, and I blasted away.

Still, Wilder gained 166 yards. He and Fencik played demolition derby all day. Gary had to have his neck and shoulders adjusted by a chiropractor after the game. Of course, when Vainisi saw Dr. Krueger taking a shower after the game, he got all upset. Couldn't that wait? Krueger does adjustments every Wednesday at Halas Hall under the watchful eye of Fred Caito. Why not today? Let Jerry hit Wilder once or twice and see if he doesn't need to have something adjusted.

MONDAY, SEPTEMBER 9, 6:30 A.M.

Called Tom in Houston for my first grade of the season. It will be no holds barred commentary— honest criticism from a coach who is going to watch every game he can, breaking down my weekly performace, and grade me A to F. "B-plus," said Williams. "Your pass defense was good, but you're still overreacting to the running play."

"What plays?" I said. "What do you mean, over-reacting?" Tom quickly put an end to my questions, pinpointing exact plays I had overrun. "Mike," he said, "any running play from sideline to sideline is yours. There's no way that boy should have gained 166 yards on you."

It was always "on *you.*" Never the defense. On you. "But he's the best back in the league," I protested.

"Sorry, Mike," came the words, "I just can't accept that."

TUESDAY, SEPTEMBER 10

We were all willing to accept the fact that New England presents a challenge. During my holdout I'd watched the Pats play a pre-season game on ESPN. "This is the team we're going to play in the Super Bowl. This is the team to beat," I told Kim. They were so talented, had outstanding quarterbacks in Steve Grogan and Tony Eason, a rugged back in Craig James, a big line, and tremendous athletic ability on defense. I was beginning to feel we might get embarrassed. So I drove over to Halas Hall and watched film. I brought a couple of reels home and took them downstairs to my damp, dark refuge with the dirty laundry, ancient card table, and single folding chair. On the walls were my goals for the season; on the floor, my $30,000 in Hydra Gym weight training equipment (I rarely work out with the team at the Halas Hall facility, preferring the peace and solitude of my basement), and my cinderblock, where I press 100 dips a day, each leg, strengthening my quad muscles, a tip I picked up from former pro Tom Graham, who told me Randy

Gradishar of the Broncos always did it. I love my basement and the privacy it provides; it's my refuge, where I can see inside myself and other teams, a place to dream my dreams of being the best.

Danny came over to watch film tonight. "You know," he said, "I never liked film until I began to see what players are really like. You get to know who's tough and who quits."

"That's right," I said.

We watched plays over and over, breaking down the blocking technique of Collins and James. Collins loves to go low on his blocks. James is just the opposite; he prefers to take you standing up. Ninety percent of the time I can jump over Collins on a blitz. James I just have to blast into. By not *studying* film most linebackers would guess wrong 50 percent of the time. I figure this film study supplies me at least a 40 percent edge—just what I need to get a shot at the quarterback.

Speaking of quarterbacks, I can see Eason is young and vulnerable, the key to beating the Pats. James has a lot of heart, and Collins will backdoor you and sneak out of the backfield if you don't keep an eye on him. Without their superstar guard, John Hannah, who's hurting, the offensive line just isn't the same. But Eason is the key.

SATURDAY, SEPTEMBER 14, 10:00 P.M.

I'm worried. Gary played real tough against Tampa Bay, and he's a streetfighting guy you want on your side Sunday. But after watching film with him tonight I'm still detecting a hesitancy on his part, a reluctance to let go. The groin injury is bothering him, he's afraid of hurting it again. Certainly he doesn't need football: he models hair mousse; is a spokesman for a bank; has his own TV show, three radio shows, and a newspaper column; is part owner of a restaurant; and has his MBA from Northwestern. I find myself thinking back to the monster hits he used to put on people—the New York Giants's Jimmy Robinson, 1977; Philly's Wally Henry in 1980—hits for which Gary earned a reputation as a "cheapshot" artist, a headhunter. He's not a cheap hitter, but because sometimes he closes his eyes before he tackles and runs in with his head down, I can see how injuries can occur. Still, Fencik works, he studies, and, most of all, he makes things happen. In the final equation, I don't think he wants to be remembered as Gary Fencik, Chicago Bear, but as Gary Fencik, businessman. Whatever it is, I'll never forget him.

After Gary left I watched another reel or two alone. I was looking for something, another key . . . and I found it. I noticed how, when Eason broke the huddle, he looked in the direction of the play. And believe it or not, one offensive lineman was so off-balance he failed to execute the proper three-point stance, tipping off every pass the Pats threw. Buddy had found the same keys I did. I've never seen him so confident before a game, thanks, in part, to a masterful game plan. He's brimming with optimism. "Execute this game plan," he told us at our meeting tonight, "and there's no way we can lose."

SUNDAY, SEPTEMBER 15, 8:00 P.M.

Well, Buddy was right. The Pats spent all of 21 seconds in our half of the field. Only once did they manage more than one first down on a drive. And all that extra film study paid off, particularly on one play when James ran a draw. As soon as I saw the backfield shift, I yelled "DRAW!" and pointed to the hole. Eason about died; he tried to audible. Too late. I creamed James at the line of scrimmage.

The guys were going nuts. "You got their plays, Samurai? What's coming next, what is next?"

"What's in the crystal ball?" Otis kept saying.

"Just listen to me," I said. "And let's keep it going." When it was over I had seven tackles, three sacks, a fumble recovery, and an interception, good enough to win the Player of the Week award.

Defensive tackle Steve McMichael, however, was also a strong candidate. He had played a terrific game, settling an old score. He was drafted by New England out of Texas in the third round in 1980, but was cut because, as Steve put it, "They wanted businessmen, not football players." He has no love lost for New England, not this down-and-dirty over-achiever we've nicknamed "Mongo" after the Alex Karras character in *Blazing Saddles* who KOs a horse with one punch. Steve loves to hunt snakes, and he and Hampton are famous for their forays into various biker taverns and pool halls, after one of which Mongo was heard to utter this legendary line: "We don't fight them pardners anymore; some of them were packing guns."

Steve is also one of the best people on the team to talk to; at the same time, he's an instigator who rarely speaks to anyone's face, but rather in a voice that appears to originate from outer space. "Yeah, I know how it is when you're making so much money" come the words, or "Man, it's hot. What the hell are we doing out here today?" When you hear something like that, you know it's McMichael. I also know he desperately wants to be an All-Pro, though he does his best to downplay it. I remember he told me, in 1982, "Singletary, guys like you and me don't make Pro Bowls. They want big-name guys. They want Hamptons, Gastineaus, Taylors, people like that."

"Steve, don't let anything like that limit your

mind," was my answer. "It may look that way now, but there's one thing about life. If you're really working, you can't be beat."

We certainly weren't beat today, not when you only allow 27 yards rushing and 179 passing (90 on one play late in the game). But Ditka's not turning cartwheels. Wilber misjudged James's speed on one play and that resulted in the 90-yard TD; and Duerson's still struggling—wondering, I think, what will happen if Todd comes back. The team reminds me of the Michael Keaton character in the movie *Mr. Mom*. When Keaton loses his job, he switches roles with his wife and stays home to do the domestic duties. Pretty soon, the laundry, cooking, and housework are piling up, toast is flying in the air, pans are overflowing. Keaton has no rhythm, no order in his life. Neither do we, despite the performance against New England. Bad timing, too. Tommy Kramer and the Minnesota Vikings are next.

TUESDAY, SEPTEMBER 17

For the first time this season, some big political footballs got tossed around today between two hardheaded, ego-driven disciples of different systems. Buddy learned his defensive strategy watching Weeb Ewbank destroy teams with a Joe Namath–led passing attack. Mike Ditka studied under George Halas and Tom Landry, men he idolizes. It's no surprise then, that Buddy and Mike have been at odds since 1982, mostly over Ditka's preference for zone defense and its turnover factor and Buddy's desire to play man to man and limit opponent yardage.

"I don't care if the defense is predictable or not; they can't stop us," Buddy would say. Buddy is also a firm believer in paying your dues; you don't just walk into his system and play. First you watch, then you learn, and *then* you play. Not so with Ditka. He subscribes to the "put your best 11 men on the field" theory of coaching and gets angry whenever Buddy excludes talented rookies because they aren't "ready" in Ryan's eyes.

"I think that's one thing a lot of coaches get hung up on today," Ditka says. "They look at someone run and decide if he can play football. If they had looked at Butkus, they would have decided he wasn't fast enough to play. That's a fallacy. It was the same with Nitschke of the Packers. In my mind, the criterion you use to evaluate a football player is 'Can he play football?' You look at character, intelligence, how he relates to his teammates, his experience, then you worry about how much he weighs and how fast he runs. That was my biggest complaint with Buddy. He downgraded kids he didn't think fit his system. I never want to lose a good football player because of coaching prejudice. That's the only way I can put it; it comes down to prejudice."

Today push came to shove, and there was no doubt in Ditka's mind where that prejudice was being placed: directly in the path of one 308-pound refrigerator named William Perry, our first-round draft choice from Clemson—"a wasted draft choice," in Buddy's oft-quoted words. Both Ditka and personnel director Bill Tobin are pushing Perry into the lineup. Fridge, the poor guy, has taken endless abuse from Day One, mostly from Hampton, who's always telling him, "Biscuit, you look hungry," calling him "Mudslide," or worse. Perry is a nice country kid, quick, but no Rhodes scholar, a kid, unfortunately, who has never worked hard in his life. The first time I saw Fridge, I told him, "You're going to have trouble with Buddy." I teased him about being lazy, doing what was expected and nothing more. "You got to work, man," I said one day after practice.

"I know, I know."

"Yeah, well come with me."

"Wha, wha, where we going?"

"To do some running, that's where." It wasn't much in the beginning, a half dozen over and backs, 40 yards or so, just enough to break a sweat. But I wanted him to understand quickly that to become a part of our defense, to be a Bear, you have to dig deeper, forget about average and start thinking exceptional.

Typically, neither Ditka nor Buddy ever minced words on the Perry issue. Why start now. Still Buddy won't budge. Not yet. "We gotta move Hampton to end; he's not an end, he's a tackle," he said. And Ditka answered, "He made All-Pro end in 1980." On and on it goes.

The second power struggle was much more enjoyable to watch. By now, my roommate, Cliff Thrift, picked up from San Diego, was telling me how patriotic I am, so it was nice when Ditka and Viking coach Bud Grant played one-upmanship with the national anthem. I read where Grant was criticizing the opposing team's sloppy behavior during the playing of the anthem, all the while praising his Vikes. Grant also chastised ABC-TV for not showing the anthem segment live. Well, if that didn't just stir up the Twin Cities, especially with the game a Thursday night special on ABC. So, Grant says, "We're going to stand out there with our feet together."

Iron Mike? Well, he never conceded anything in his life, so why start now? After all, this is the man who once said, "One on one. You and me. Let's see who's tougher. I lived for competition. Every game was a personal affront. Everything in my life was based on beating the other guy." Well, this time, the other guy not only happens to be a great coach, but one who was once heard to utter, "It's not what you know but who you know" after Halas hired Ditka in 1982. In other words, no love lost here. So Ditka says to the team, "We're going to stand there. I want your feet together. I want your helmets under your left arm. And I want your hand on your chest over your heart. We'll fix them. Let's see who has more class. That's the way we're going to do it." And that's just what we did—for the rest of the reason. Touché.

Of course, it's a pity Kramer couldn't have played the game in that position, because I sense he was going to be trouble. Sure, he had two tough, elusive runners in the backfield in Darrin Nelson and Ted Brown, a potential All-Pro receiver in Anthony Carter, and a rugged, opportunistic defense that dined on turnovers. But Kramer was the key. He's their McMahon, a survivalist, a leader. Unfortunately, our leader, McMahon, will be sitting this dance out, hurting, as he is, with a bad back and infected leg. He spent most of Wednesday sitting in the stands with Joe Namath, his childhood hero.

Me? I was feeling more and more obsessed by the minute. "This is the biggest game of our life," I told Kim. "Mike, you said that last week," she said, "and the week before that." So I did. But this week I mean it, and it's showing up in practice where I got into a couple of "misunderstandings" with my teammates and I'm cussing a blue streak. Danny Rains told Kim, about my foul mouth and she chewed me out. "With your testimony, you really ruined it," she said. It didn't help matters much that I walked in two hours late for dinner with five reels of film. But I can't get Kramer off my mind. He's just too good, too dangerous.

THURSDAY, SEPTEMBER 19
"Why can't you guys stop this?" It's Hampton again, pissed off that Kramer's throwing strikes all over the Metrodome, embarrassing us on national TV. Short, long, in, out, over, under. Every time we get a guy in his face, he throws a complete pass.

"You guys in back," yelled Hampton, "hey, you gotta do your part. I'm getting the shit beat out of me up here. What are you doing?"

"We're trying to do our jobs," said Leslie. "You guys have got to get to him."

Me? I'm refereeing this debate, trying to get the game under control. We were down 17–9 early in the third quarter and McMahon out, the offense struggling under Steve Fuller. Steve's a great guy, the perfect backup quarterback. He even looks like a quarterback, Rhodes scholar, always carrying a briefcase, nicely dressed. He's the perfect guy to have at the helm when you're ahead and need to milk the clock. He audibles well, takes control out there, and is, in my view, the best number two quarterback in the league. But when you're behind and the offense needs motivation, Jim has that innate ability to demand respect from his line and get it, especially guys like Van Horne and our starting right guard, Kurt Becker.

Becker, 6'5", 267 pounds, is a little off cue, a punk rock devotee who sets the tone for the entire line. He's a Michigan man, very smart, cool, glib, great with the guys. And he's always messing with Van Horne, egging him on. Deep down I think Keith's a mellow southern Californian, but Becker just won't allow it; he has Van Horne constantly living on the edge.

The rest of the line are no shrinking violets, either. I think it's the meanest, toughest, best offensive line in all of football, lunch-bucket guys who mirror their beloved offensive line coach, Dick Stanfel, who plays the part of the grumpy, fog-horned father figure to perfection. In a way, Stanfel, at 58, symbolizes our entire assistant coaching staff, the oldest, most experienced and—I believe—the best in the league. Watching this group work without a single day off from July to January, breaking down film, grading plays, picking apart a team, is like watching nine-part harmony. Nine men, each with individual duties, working like pistons in an engine, individual but always pushing the car forward. Their goal is to make us better players, to provide us with the instruction and information we need to win. And Stanfel knows all about winning. He's the son of an immigrant, a man who fed his family by working with his hands—a coal miner, boxer, steelworker, cowpoke. A man so poor that when a boss once wrote *Stanfel* on his paycheck—the real family surname was Stamfelj—the old man never argued. He just kept the new name. His son would go on to become a four-time All-Pro guard and the first offensive lineman to win a league MVP award for his play in 1959 in leading Detroit to a title. Every Thursday after practice now, Stanfel shuffles off with Van Horne, Becker, and the rest of his boys for a beer or two—or 10—at a local tavern. He treats all his linemen like the man he is, and they love him for it.

The guy who improved most under Stanfel has to be center Jay Hilgenberg. I respect Jay so much, maybe because he's a lot like me—worked for all he's got. He grew up in Iowa, wrestling in high school and college (where he was a two-time All-American) and making All-Big 10 honorable mention in football. But Jay never got drafted, and it hurt him. He spent his first three years around here feeling a little sorry for himself, wondering if he was good enough to play. Then, in 1984, it seems he dedicated himself in the weight room and after practice to being the best in the game. It showed. His strength, running ability, and technique (he has great hands) have all improved to all-pro level.

Two of the toughest guys on the team are Mark Bortz, our right guard, and Jimbo Covert, our right tackle. Bortzy has to have the hardest head in the world. We call him the "Dome." He also has two of the longest arms and as a converted defensive end uses them to full advantage, especially in the trenches. Jimbo, well, he reminds me of a farmer with a corncob pipe in his mouth. Some guys get on him about his image, calling him "Jumbo" because he's so low-key, so gentle off the field. But believe me, during a game, you don't want to deal with him. He's very, very physical, and he'll take that part of the game as far as you want to go.

But right now, during halftime of this massacre, we're just trying to stay alive. McMahon has been bugging Ditka to play. Finally, in the third quarter, Ditka relents. "All right, son, get in there," he says. Jim rolled into the game like a gunfighter strutting into Dodge City. You could just see the whole offense pick up.

I first met Jim during his BYU days, at a Kodak All-American function, where he and Scott Woerner, a safety from Georgia, were raising hell. It's not that Jim didn't have class; he just did what he wanted when he wanted. Like the night of the All-American banquet, he and Woerner were drinking beer, wearing sunglasses, flipping the bird to anyone and everyone who came near the table. To me, Jim's always been like that Merrill Lynch ad—a breed apart—a lewd, crude character who seems to be cast into the Bears straight out of a *Mad Max* picture. Definitely, he's a catalyst to our club.

Catalyst, smatalyst, what he did tonight was beyond belief! Three touchdown passes in less than seven minutes. Boom, Gault 70 yards for a touchdown. Boom, Dennis McKinnon 25 yards for a touchdown. Boom, another pass to McKinnon (43 yards) for six. Final score: Bears 33, Vikings 24. It was the first time in 16 years that two Bear receivers went over 100 yards receiving in the same game. McMahon was wild in the dressing room, drinking beer, laughing, soaking up all the adulation. I'm happy, don't get me wrong, but Kramer was 28 for 55, 436 yards, and three touchdowns. "Too much zone," said Buddy. "I'd like to see us play it more," said Ditka. Great, they sound like Hampton and Frazier.

Report card: "The inside linemen did a good job, but your tight end coverage was sloppy." said Tom Williams. "You're making the wrong turn when you look back for the ball. You're not ready; you're looking at the quarterback instead of the receiver. A—."

WEDNESDAY, SEPTEMBER 26, 9:00 A.M.

Time for twenty questions, or, should I say, 120 questions. Buddy and I have played this game for four years now, breaking down film, me on one side of his desk, Buddy on the other, the projector always separating us. It's my job to supply answers to his defensive calls. On any given week, we could have a half-dozen or more basic formations and, as I said, dozens of variable coverages.

"AFC," said Buddy.

It was a Redskins film, this week's upcoming opponent. The Big Bad 'Skins, revenge time for their 23–19 loss to us last year in the playoffs. Already Dexter Manley, their mohawked lineman, is popping off, saying they're going to intimidate us, knock Walter out of the game. Mistake. Otis is fired up. So is Ditka. He told us today, "Fellas, we got a team that's gonna come in here, into our backyard, and try to intimidate us. They said they were going to intimidate *us*." His face was fire-engine red, veins popping out of his neck. *"What are we going to say about that? I don't know about you, but I'd say it's going to be pretty tough. . . ."*

"C'mon, Samurai, AFC."

I double-checked the coverage, knowing Buddy's mental clock was ticking. "Seventeen, Willie," I said, alluding to our basic 4–3 defense, with Cover 2 (man to man).

"OK. Three-four," said Buddy. "C'mon, hurry up, hurry up."

"Sam Blitz." That meant, depending on the strength of the formation, where the tight end lined up, either Otis or Wilber was blitzing.

It went on and on for two hours. We've got the 50 Blitz (that's me), or Pudding (me again), or Peaches (Duerson on a blitz) or a 45-Blitz (Fencik up the gut), all solid, perfect for a week in which we've got a big mountain to climb.

Every season in the NFL, another game is played off the field, where up-and-coming teams such as the Bears try to crawl over the elite—the Cowboys, the 49ers, the Redskins. We took a small step last week, beating Minnesota on the road. At the moment, our offense is ranked number one in the league, and if we can beat Washington, we'll be 4–0 for the first time since 1963. To do so means crawling over a team that has tremendous pride, a great coach, and quality athletes, heroes in a city that, much like Chicago, supports and respects its ballplayers. But now we have their address, and it was about time to give them a call.

THURSDAY, SEPTEMEBER 26, 11:00 A.M.

There's a thickness in the air. You can taste it. Some games are going to be battles, others knock-down, drag-out wars. This is a war. I love it! Let's get it on. I wish Todd were here. Games like this we'd just look at each other, nod, and say, "See you after the game, I'm going to work."

Tom Thayer will replace Becker at right guard; we lost Beck for the year with a severe knee injury in the Minnesota game. Tom's a guy who demands respect; anyone who can play 27 straight games in a one-year period since coming to the Bears from the USFL Arizona Wranglers deserves more than a passing nod. Not that Tom jokes or punks out like Becker. He prefers instead to pump up in the weight room where he trains every day. At 6'4", 261 pounds, he's got great size for a guard, and, believe me, he'll need every bit of it this week. He makes his first NFL start against the Redskins' defensive tackle Dave Butz, who at 6'7", 300 pounds is the size of a small planet.

In meetings, Haupt's been firing off his rat-a-tat commentary, biting off his words in a clipped cadence. Imagine Patton's speech pattern on fast forward and you'll get a feel for this former Packer guard.

"Hampton, you're getting your butt beat out there," he screamed today. "Dent, you gotta come off the ball! Steve, I hope you're not going to have another game like last week—you got your ass kicked."

A couple of us started to snicker. Haupt's voice was just too much to take. "It's not funny, you guys; it's not funny when you're *getting your butts kicked like that!*"

I watched a lot of film alone, keying on quarterback Joe Theismann, seeing a guy who is very disciplined, very sharp, but when disappointed very temperamental. When plays break down or balls are dropped, he gets very upset at his players. It's a weakness we want to exploit. After Theismann, John

Riggins and George Rogers, their two running backs, are the keys. I'd watched the Houston game, seeing, *boom*, one play after another. Riggins up the gut. *Boom!* Rogers off tackle, pounding up and down the field. It's nasty, in-your-face football, and, with that huge line up front, the Redskins play it better than almost anyone in the league.

SUNDAY, SEPTEMBER 29, 7:00 P.M.

Unfortunately, that's just what the 'Skins did against us in the first half today, leading 10–0 at intermission. Buddy was so upset he was seeing stars. "Hey, if we keep this up, we might as well go out and be a doormat. We're going to have to suck it up, and our special teams had better do something. They're killing us with theirs."

But this is the kind of season it's turning out to be: first play of the second half, Willie Gault busts out of the blocks, gets great blocks from Shaun Gayle and Dennis Gentry, and goes 99 yards for a touchdown, the longest kickoff return in the history of Soldier Field. It's beginning to look like Mission Impossible around here, every week a new hero. And it couldn't have happened at a better time for Willie—"Hollywood" as we call him, because he's always checking out his hair, his clothes, talking about deals, agents, producers he's met out West. That's hurt Willie's image on the team, in the sense that he's perceived by many players as a kid who's not interested in reaching his potential, not willing to pay the price to improve. Willie loves the limelight and wants to be respected, but as yet he hasn't put in the time. His speed is unbelievable; nobody can stay with him. But catching 40 passes his first season may have hurt him. He downshifted a bit in 1984, catching just 34 balls, and the prevailing sentiment is if he's not careful, he could lose both

Hollywood and his football career. A lot of guys
don't want to deal with him, but I like Willie; we talk
a lot after practice when we run. I tell him he needs
to concentrate, to prove to the guys that he can take
a hit, that he's willing to test the middle of the field.
I just see him as a guy who thinks he knows what he
wants but, in truth, at this point is missing it.

Yet he sure kept us alive today, long enough for
our offense to explode for a team-record 31 points
in the third quarter. The biggest play may have been
a fourth and one, Washington driving, when Mike
Richardson and Wilber stacked up Riggins for no
gain. Stopped him cold. In a way, Mike typifies so
many professional athletes—marvelous physical
specimens, cooly confident, but contented, it seems,
to play really a shade below their true abilities. I've
always felt that if Mike buckled down, took a hard,
long look inside himself and made a commitment to
be the best cornerback in the N.F.L., he'd been in a
class by himself. He's that good. But first he has to
decide what he wants both in and out of football. Is
he content to be a starter? To charm the ladies? (He
and Dent are far and way the team leaders in that
category). Or to set goals, to push himself past the
competition. Wilber's coming on, too, getting better
all the time. "Mike," he told me before the game,
"I'm trying to get there, to do the things I've got to
get done, but it's tough. I think everyone expects
you to make mistakes in your second year, but I
don't want to make any."

"Don't worry. You're doing a great job, more than
anyone could ask for," I said. "The worst thing you
can do now is look at negatives. If you do, it will set
the tone for the day and affect your play."

Manley also got a large dose of his own medicine
today, courtesy of offensive tackle Andy Frederick.
Andy stepped in for the injured Covert and did an
outstanding job. Andy came over to Chicago from

Cleveland in 1983, and I don't think he's said 200 words since he got here. He never complains. In fact, you can barely tell when he's talking because he doesn't move his lips. He talks through his teeth. But at 6'6", 265 pounds, he's happy letting his actions speak loudest. I think Manley got an earful today. So did the defense, courtesy of Herr Ryan's postgame comments.

"Well, we're 4–0, but I'll guarantee you it's not because of anyone in this group. Those guys over there are packing us right now. Don't let anybody blow smoke up your butt. Understand what the situation is."

MONDAY, SEPTEMBER 30, 11:30 P.M.

"Michael, this phone is driving me crazy," Kim said.

Can't say I blame her. It starts ringing now at 7:00 A.M. and stops only because we turn on the answering machine at 11:00 P.M. Even so, when we wake up the next morning, there's always two or three more messages. When the phone isn't ringing, we often sit in bed and talk about the turn of events, trying to keep our life in perspective. The pressure is building with each win.

"If you think about it," I said to Kim, "this is all so short-lived—four, five years at the most. I'd much rather put up with this than what we faced in the early days. Remember how blessed we are compared to our days back in school when we went on walks for dates."

That seemed to soften her up a bit. "Remember how we used to spend your laundry money—all $30 of it—on dinner after a game?" Kim said. "Or I'd spend all my job money on a new polo shirt for you?"

Speaking of ring, yesterday after the game, McMichael was offering two free tickets for tonight's wrestling spectacular at the Horizon. Live! The

Hulkster! Danny's a diehard fan, so he convinced me to go. Mistake. I've been a pro wrestling fan since I was in the ninth grade, but the place went up for grabs when we walked in. They kept shouting, "Samurai," mobbing us for autographs, getting all pumped up over the Redskins victory. They even gave us a standing ovation, which, I don't mind telling you, sent a chill down my spine. But when it got out of hand, the security guards saved us, taking us down near ringside, where we sat across from Mr. T, who looks about the size of Mr. P, William Perry. It was a great show, but I don't think I'll be viewing any more grudge matches. Not as long as we keep winning the ones we're playing on Sunday.

"When Walter spoke I knew it was from the heart. 'Mike, I've been through so much. Every time you turn around, somebody wants your time. They want you to do this, they want you to do that. Sometimes it gets to you. It's hard to find a friend because you start thinking people want to be your friend because you're Walter Payton.' "

8
OCTOBER 1985

The colors are beginning to change, and a warm wind blows this time of year. Fall in Chicago has a flavor all its own. Unfortunately, the winds of change seem to be blowing right past Halas Hall this week. We're still living in the past, waiting, wondering when—or if—Todd and Al are going to return. Nothing served to symbolize that better than the scene during our film study.

Buddy turned on the light, and the first thing we saw was Todd.

"Taco!" Buddy cried and started hugging him. Then came the flurry of questions: "You back, man?" "What's the deal?"

"Man, you just can't win," Todd said. "I give up."

I was happy and sad all at once. I'd figured Todd finally had given up his year-long fight for a bigger contract and was coming into camp on Bear terms. His loss would be our gain. But that's not why Todd was here. "I just came in to clean out my locker," he said.

I could feel the tears welling up in my eyes, so when he walked out I couldn't sit still. I left the room, heading upstairs to the locker room to head home. But once in my truck, I couldn't move. I just sat, listening to music, my senses dulled. I waited for Todd. Finally, he emerged from Halas Hall.

"How you doing?" I asked.

"Doin' good."

"You're looking well."

"I'm tryin'."

"Got a place to stay?"

He said Willie was putting him up. I was hurt; I thought he should have called, and I told him so. He told me he had just arrived from his hometown of Columbus, Ohio. "Well, if you need anything, give me a call, anytime, anywhere. You can count on me." He turned to walk away; it was getting late.

"Todd."

He turned around.

"I love you. Take care and God Bless."

That was the last time I saw Todd Bell.

Losing Todd only added to our misery. Spirits are not too high around here anyway. We're getting sick of seeing the Tampa Bay film. On Tuesday, it was the whole game, Wednesday just the first half, Thursday the second half. We're sick of it. So today, Friday, we decided to play a little trick on Buddy. When he walked in with the two cans of film, we knew that the red can was our game against Tampa Bay, the green a game the Bucs had played against someone else. When Buddy left the room, Hampton grabbed the red canister and stuck it under Buddy's desk. No good. We needed a better hiding place. So I took it and tossed it in the trash.

"OK, close the lights," said Buddy, returning to the scene of the crime.

Argh! It was Tampa Bay again!

"Samurai, thought you got away with something, didn't you?" laughed Buddy. He had figured we'd try something so he put the Bucs' film in the green canister. The old switch-er-roo. Fooled us all again!

Still, playing hide-the-film-canister is a pretty dangerous maneuver for a man whose wife once made a marriage vow that said she would "keep you from acting 60 until you are 60." It was an obvious reference to my "mature" tastes, the fact I wear ugly shoes because they offer good support, make sure Kim buttons up before leaving the house, and relate better to her 70-year-old grandfather than to any of our friends. "Mike, don't be so boring. You act like an old man," she's constantly telling me.

Like tonight. Kim's old boss was moving out of town, and she wanted to have one last dinner with him. I pushed for a nice quiet movie. I love movies, but she won, reminding me on the way to the restaurant to "make sure you talk," fully aware of my tendency to deliver monosyllabic answers to questions such as "How's the season going?" ("Fine.")

I guess it all dates back to my wanting to lead, wanting to do the "right" things all the time: not to drink, to try to inspire others by example. I tell the guys I'll do anything I can for them. Just call. Anytime. "But Mike," says Kim, "sometimes you just have to let go and let them see you can have fun, too."

SUNDAY, OCTOBER 6, AIRBORNE, 7:00 P.M.

Had a heck of a time holding James Wilder in check today, but we did, limiting him to 29 yards in 18 carries, very satisfying since Wilder was working on his seventh straight 100-yard game (dating back to the 1984–85 season). But once again, we needed a comeback to win. McMahon stunk up the joint in the first half, playing catch with McKinnon's toes. Consequently, we trailed 12–3 in the third quarter before Duerson picked off a pass by DeBerg to set up a 21-yard TD pass from McMahon to McKinnon. Walter then scored our last two TDs in an eventual 27–19 victory. Duerson, however, made the big difference. He's really coming on, living up to his reputation as one of the smartest guys on the club. Dave's a one-man band with the brass instruments and once toured around the world with one large group. He's also been a law clerk and worked in Washington for a U.S. senator and he's already formed his own drug and alcohol awareness program for kids. At the beginning of the season, I thought he might not have the nose for the game; I questioned his toughness. But right now, he's hitting hard, putting fear into the minds of both running backs and tight ends.

Speaking of tight ends, Emery Moorehead had a big game—eight catches, 114 yards, including seven receptions in the second half. That tied him with a now-arthritic-hipped Bear for most catches in one game. Emery is an unsung hero, a guy who hustles every step of the way, a selfless sort who plays wherever the club needs him. He was a running back with the Broncos and Giants before coming to Chicago in 1981. In four years, he's caught more than 100 balls.

MONDAY, OCTOBER 7, 6:45 A.M.

I'm pumped up, boasting to Williams how we stopped Wilder. "Sure, the line overpowered Tampa Bay," he said. "But it wasn't so much what you did. And, oh, by the way, you didn't fill a hole. It's one play, but if you're going to be the best . . . A—."

Before he hung up, Williams made sure he destroyed my day. He told me Buddy wasn't long for the Bears. "The guy's too good a motivator," he said. "A guy like that wants to be a head coach."

"No, he doesn't want to be a head coach," I said, not wanting to believe it.

"I don't know," Tom said. "I just don't think you can keep him."

TUESDAY, OCTOBER 8

Had a rollicking roast tonight for former Bear Jim Osborne, who retired last year after 13 seasons on the defensive line. McMahon, Walter, Hampton, Buddy, and I were on the dais; Mike Adamle hosted, and it was brutal. The main theme centered on how Jim was the ugliest guy in the history of the free world, how those couldn't possibly be his kids, how he had to pay his wife to marry him. He was so ugly that . . . well, you get the picture.

When it came time for me to rake Ozzy over the coals, I just didn't have the heart. First of all, I'm no Don Rickles (hard to tell, I know), and secondly, Jim was so inspirational in my early battles with Buddy. I remember one bit of advice in particular: "Mike," Ozzy told me, "there's one thing you have to understand about Buddy. Don't ever cheat on him. If he tells you, particularly if you're a rookie, to touch the line on wind sprints, touch the line. Not one centimeter away. The line. Believe me, he'll be watching. And keep your mouth shut. If you do that, one day you'll realize Buddy will be one of your closest friends."

Still, when I got up, Hampton looked at me. "Don't be nice, Samurai," he said. "Well," I began, "the toughest part has been done. I just don't have any bad things to say. My major reason for coming tonight was to thank Ozzy for all the things he's done for me. A lot of times I was unsure, needed someone to talk to, a shoulder to cry on, and Ozzy was always there. I just want everyone to know that no matter where I am, if someone mentions Ozzy's name in bad fashion, you're going to have to deal with me." I turned to Ozzy. "Oz, remember this," I said. "No matter where you are, what you do, if you ever need me, just give me a call."

Speaking of calls, San Francisco's on the line this week. Another hill to climb, another step up the ladder. The 49ers are one of the elite, defending Super Bowl champions, no, *the* elite—as smart and sophisticated a club as there is in the league, thanks to their coach, Bill Walsh, who leaves no stone unturned in preparing his team, both mentally and physically. More than any other NFL coach, Walsh takes a high-tech approach to game-plan preparation. I think he has the most modernistic and innovative mind in the game today. As for his quarterback, Joe Montana, well, I respect him more than just about anybody else in the league, his toughness, scrambling ability, his accurate arm. His receiver, Dwight Clark, is no picnic either. Sure, he's slower than most wide outs, but once the game begins, Clark's like a ghost. Every time you turn around he's slipping into a zone, running free along the back line of the end zone, or doing a dance along the sideline before running out of bounds in front of the first-down marker. The Niners line also features three All-Pros, and Roger Craig has blossomed into one of the most versatile and dangerous all-purpose backs in the league. For all those reasons, our game plan this week ran to 60 pages—a new high. As usual, Buddy is playing mind games in it, psyching up different guys. Typically, Otis got top billing; he gets a paragraph or two almost every week; so does Hampton. Both have fragile egos and need a weekly booster shot for their confidence. This week Buddy is telling Otis, "We've got to have a great game from you; no ifs, ands, or buts about it. You've got to go in there and tear up everything. I know you can do it."

Buddy is a lot like Ditka in the sense he knows how to motivate every man on his team. With Dent, for example, Buddy takes a different tack. He likes to berate Richard, to ridicule his play. "Don't let them run over you again like they did that last time," he wrote in the game plan. "Don't let them drag you 10 yards downfield. We can't have that this week."

On Wednesday, after practice, I made sure the fellas knew where Samurai stood on the San Francisco issue. "We have to rededicate ourselves to where we're going to be the rest of the year," I said. "There's no reason we can't be one of the best defenses in the league, if not number one. Right now we're 12th, and it stinks. The next game is going to prove where we are. Either we're going to be great or not. Let's make up our minds. Forget Al and Todd coming back this season. Whatever happens is going to happen. We can't control it. We just have to stay together and help each other more than we are now."

It's time to prove we belong. To everyone. The press, our fans, the rest of the league. The local writers and TV people are about half on the bandwagon. I think they sense that as a team we don't know yet if we're any good or not. Dave and Wilber's adjustments are the most obvious. With Todd, I'd just yell, "Cover me, back me up," and he knew instinctively what to do. With Dave, sometimes the answer is "Cover what?" By then, the play is over. Communication is everything in the 46. When I don't hear Otis or Wilber yelling, "Watch the tight end," or "Who's got the back?" I'm worried, fearful someone's either missed an audible or isn't focused fully on the impending play.

After practice, I ran again with the Fridge. Lately, Haupt has been doing his drill-sergeant number on Fridge. "C'mon, Fridge, get a move on, get it going." Up-downs, sleds, running, drills till you drop. But now Fridge is getting into it, asking *me* now when we're going to run. I had him doing some drills for me, making like a guard or a fullback coming off the ball, giving me different looks out of the backfield. I even had him impersonate a running back making an option pass. While we were working out, a funny thing happened: Ditka strolled by, puffing away on his postpractice cigar, wiggling it around his mouth like a modern-day Groucho Marx. Ditka wants Fridge in the lineup—somewhere, anywhere. Last week he inserted him into the kickoff coverage team, and the kid responded with two tackles. But that's nothing compared to what Ditka's thinking now.

"Think you can run with that thing?" he said, still wiggling the cigar. Fridge's face lit up like a Christmas tree. "Oh yeah," he said, "Oh yeah! I can do it. I can do it!" Ditka didn't say anything. He just kept on walking. But he sure did have a funny smile on his face.

Our locker room would never be confused with a Christian Science Reading Room. Walter, Mr. Soul Train dance finalist himself, is the master of ceremonies in this show. Walter is the disc jockey, supplying the boom box and tapes of whatever is the latest greatest hit. Last year it was Madonna, and the song was "Superstar" (can't see why he liked it, can you?). McMichael loved that song. He'd strut into the room, chest out, point a finger at Walter, and scream out, "Hey, Walter, hit it." On would go the music, and the place would start jamming. This year, it's Billy Ocean's "When the Going Gets Tough, the Tough Get Going." Man,

Walter flips that on, and the place starts rocking.
Every other week, McMichael slaps his arms real
loud, screaming bloody murder in the middle of the
room.

SUNDAY, OCTOBER 13, 9:00 P.M.

Today the joint was jumping. We were ready for the
49ers. I looked around the locker room, saw Horne
and Becker hanging out. Hilgenberg, Bortzy, Reggie
Phillips, Ken Taylor, our two young DBs, rookies
hoping to get their shot. I sat there, letting my eyes
and mind wander, looking at my teammates, some
here only a year, too young to remember the climb,
the depressing 1970s and early 1980s, others in
from Day One. It's an eclectic group. Take Tom
Andrews, a 6'4", 267-pound tackle-center in his
second year out of Louisville. He was a geography
major in college, but that didn't help him find his
way home one night when the offensive line went
downtown to do the Ditka show and left him there.
He was screaming at his linemates the next day,
calling them all sorts of names, but he was quick to
forgive and forget. That's just the kind of kid he is—
the kind any mother or father would be proud to
have.

Then there's Tim Wrightman, 6'3", 237-pounds,
first player to sign with the USFL, unanimous All-
American at UCLA. You look at him and think, why
in the world is he playing football? The man should
be on the beach modeling swimwear. He reminds
me of Ditka. Tim doesn't have the greatest speed,
but he has great hands, and he'll run over you as
soon as look at ya. I've seen linebackers and DBs
fold up like accordions after hitting Tim. He never
gives up.

And what about Stefan Humphries, our 6'3", 263-
pound All-American guard from Michigan, who was

a Rhodes scholar candidate with a 3.77 in BioEngineering. He played with Becker on the same U of M line. This spring, Stefan's enrolled in Northwestern Medical School. I caught myself thinking about my first year at Baylor, premed, making Cs, doing my darndest to stay alive. Stefan was premed all through school, and I'll guarantee you he's a player of the future around here. He wants to be the best, yet at the same time, his eyes are open, looking ahead. Stefan wants it all. And he's going to get it.

Calvin Thomas, the Rich Little of the Bears, has been around four years now, backing up Matt Suhey, sparking our special teams. But I think he's definitely in the wrong business. He should be on stage. He can mock anyone on the team, and yet he has a very serious side. He's a history buff, and both he and Becker have serious tempers. Don't mess with Calvin unless you're ready to do some dealin'.

Another guy who broke in with Calvin is Dennis Gentry, my old teammate from Baylor, Dennis the Menace. The second leading rusher in Baylor history, behind Walter Abercrombie, he led the club in special team hits in 1983. Dennis definitely was not the greatest student in college, truly ambivalent about education, but in the last year he's taken life and football far more seriously. People underestimate him because of his size (5'8", 181 pounds), but he'll hit you. I know. Dennis is the guy I broke several helmets on at Baylor.

Then there's Thomas Sanders, who made the club as a 9th-round draft choice this year. Thomas is scary. He wasn't supposed to play his senior season at Texas A&M because of a herniated disk in his back, but he still led the team in rushing. He's got all the ability in the world and one day may replace Walter when Sweetness decides he's had enough. The only thing about Thomas, maybe, is he needs to work a little more in the off-season, prepare himself

(Photo by Chris Hansen)

At Baylor, I had a bead on the ballcarriers, earning league defensive MVP award an unprecedented three straight seasons, making more than 600 tackles in four seasons.

(Photo by Chris Hansen)

Coach Teaff reached out to all his players, giving another meaning to the word winning.

(Photo courtesy North Texas State Sports Information Department)

Before becoming head coach at North Texas State, Corky Nelson helped make my life miserable at Baylor, and I thank him for it today. He never let up, telling me "You'll do what I say, when I say it, and how I say it." Without him, I'd have never made the pros.

(Photo courtesty Kodak)

Selected by the American Football Coaches Association

KODAK ALL AMERICA TEAM · A.F.C.A.

Top Row *(left to right):*
Ken Easley, Defensive Back, UCLA
Mark May, Offensive Lineman, Pittsburgh
John Scully, Center, Notre Dame
David Young, Tight End, Purdue
Bill Dugan, Offensive Lineman, Penn State
Leonard Mitchell, Defensive Lineman, Houston
Louis Oubre, Offensive Lineman, Oklahoma
Mike Singletary, Linebacker, Baylor

Middle Row *(left to right):*
Hugh Green, Defensive Lineman, Pittsburgh
E. J. Junior, Defensive Lineman, Alabama
Nick Eyre, Offensive Lineman, Brigham Young
Lawrence Taylor, Defensive Lineman, North Carolina
Mark Herrmann, Quarterback, Purdue
Ron Simmons, Defensive Lineman, Florida State
Bob Crable, Linebacker, Notre Dame
Ron Lott, Defensive Back, Southern California

Front Row *(left to right):*
Herschel Walker, Running Back, Georgia
Jarvis Redwine, Running Back, Nebraska
Jim McMahon, Quarterback, Brigham Young
George Rogers, Running Back, South Carolina
John Simmons, Defensive Back, Southern Methodist
Scott Woerner, Defensive Back, Georgia
Ken Margerum, Wide Receiver, Stanford

That's me, top row right, along with some future all-pros, including Herschel Walker (34), McMahon (9), Hugh Green (39), E. J. Junior (39), Lawrence Taylor (98), Ronnie Lott (second row, right), and Kenny Easley (5). That's McMahon's party mate in the first row, madman Margerum (28).

Left: Reverend Charles Singletary, a large imposing presence who worked hard, but was exposed to temptation and submitted to it. *Below:* Grady Singletary, who took over as the father-figure in my life before his devastating death at age 22, killed by a drunk driver.

Opposite page, clockwise from top: My mother Rudell Singletary, the rock to which our family always turned; some of the Singletary clan, just hangin' out; and finally, me at age nine, free at last from childhood sickness, doing some exploring on Woodward Street.

It only takes one look to see the inner strength of my Worthing High School coach Oliver Brown. Whether it was in the classroo or on the football field, Brown had one golden rule: "Remember, son," he said, "don't take any shortcuts."

As the season wore on, I
found myself pulling
closer and closer to my
roomie, Cliff Thrift, who
had overcome a streak of
bad luck to make a big
impact on special teams
for the Bears.

(Photos by Jonathan Daniel)

When we play on Sundays, I
picture old people getting
well, young kids waking up
with smiles on their face.

Mr. Dance Fever finalist himself, Walter Payton, is really two men in one. A smiling, practical-joker on the field, he fiercely guards his privacy and is subjected to strong moods off the field.

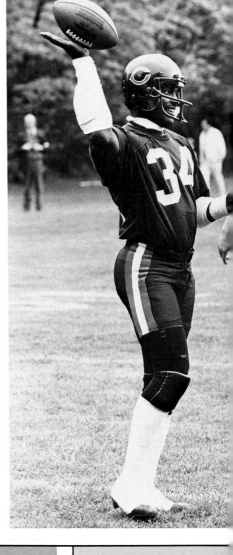

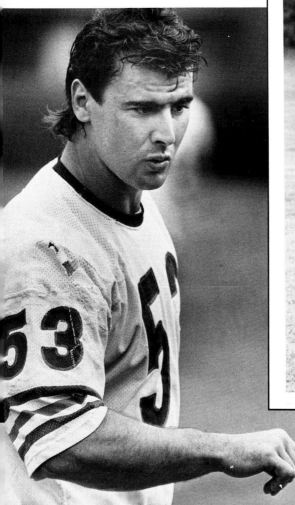

Discovered by the Bears on a minor league game film, linebacker Danny Rains has grown into one of my closest and most trusted friends on the team.

The brightest smile and fastest feet on the Bears belong to Willie "Hollywood" Gault, who sometimes lets his love of the good life and the fast track to cinema success get in the way of becoming a great football player.

The eyes have it. And in the playoffs nobody wanted it more than me.

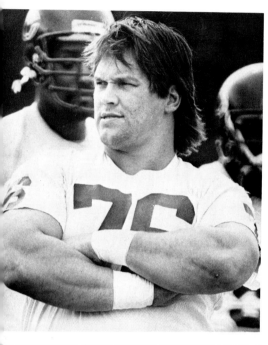

Team leaders come in all shapes and sizes. Here are two sides of defensive tackle Steve McMichael, who loves to mix it up, opponents and otherwise, and has never had an ounce of quit in him.

(Photos by Jonathan Daniel)

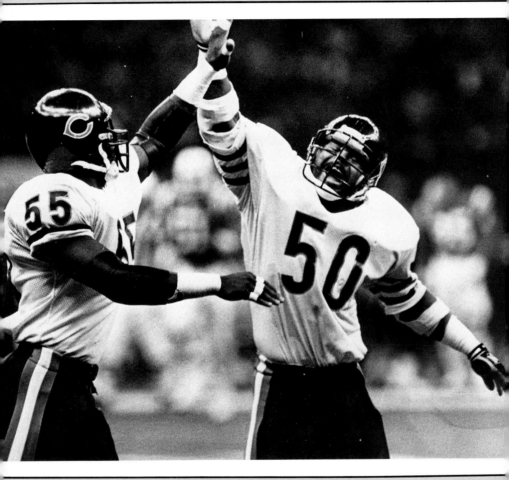

In the Super Bowl, Otis and I couldn't resist a little
high-level communication.

(Photo by Jonathan Daniel)

The Big O. It was a long journey from Brooklyn to the big time. Sometimes I felt Otis had lost his way, wasn't sure, or didn't care about his future. But I've always loved Otis like a brother— a feeling that will never change.

You only have to play with—or against—Jimbo Covert once to know that he'll do whatever it takes to win. In my book, he's one of the top five Bears and one of the finest offensive linemen in the NFL today.

You wanted to cry when they helped Leslie off the field in the Super Bowl, but hard work and lots of prayer have given us high hopes that No. 21 will be back on the field before the end of 1986.

(Photo by Jonathan Danie

Sometimes, even in a game, you need to bend down and ask for a little guidance.

(Photos by Jonathan Daniel)

When McMahon mocked NFL commissioner Pete Roselle with this headband during the Rams' playoff, it made us all proud. Jim may be crazy but I'll tell you one thing: We're sure glad he's on our side.

Is love a four-letter word in the NFL? Well, no matter, because the defense all loved Buddy Ryan, who slowly grew into a father-figure for me after years of ridicule and complaint during the days of Neill Armstrong.

(Photos by Jonathan Daniel)

The toughest interior designer in the NFL, Wilber Marshall slowly discovered that only through hard work and dedication was he going to become a part of the Buddy System. And when he did, there was no stopping him.

(Photos by Jonathan Daniel)

Leaving a myriad of personal projects and concern over reinjuring his groin behind, Gary Fencik showed us the way to the Super Bowl.

Playing in pain has become a way of life for Dan Hampton. Fortunately, when the season ends, Dan quickly retreats to the life he really loves— farming in Arkansas.

Opposite: During a 36–0 shutout of the Atlanta Falcons, Otis, who played like a man possessed, and I had a little meeting of the minds.

(Photos by Jonathan Daniel)

The dangerous Mr. Dickerson seems to attract a crowd wherever he goes. In the NFC Championship Dickerson found out the true meaning of the song "When the Going Gets Tough, the Tough Get Going." On this play, we were all going right into his face.

(Photo by Jonathan Daniel)

Mr. P. himself, The Fridge, sporting the face, the smile,
and the figure that spawned a certifiable phenomenon.
Now, if he could only stay awake during film sessions . . .

Burdened by an inequitable contract, the Colonel, Richard Dent, finally shed his concerns late in the season, to manhandle both the Giants and Rams in playoff games and win the MVP award in Super Bowl XX.

(Photo by Jonathan Daniel)

Content to be just another center during his first two years with the Bears, Jay Hilgenberg buckled down, pumped the weights, and quickly became one of the most dominant offensive linemen in the game.

(Photos by Jonathan Daniel)

On and off the field Walter Payton still attracts a crowd.

Mike Ditka made his point clear from Day One: "I want football players." His golden rule is that you play by his.

The captain of my home team, Kim is the driving force behind everything I do.

against injury. He's already been hurt a lot here. If he can stabilize, he's going to be very, very good.

Ken Margerum. The madman. I remember the first time I saw him was when I was still in college at the Kodak All-America dinner. Ken was one of the rowdiest, craziest guys I'd ever seen in my life. We were all sitting down at the banquet, and he and McMichael were drinking like there was no tomorrow. Ken picked up a fish, stared it straight in the eye, then bit its head off. Then he spit it out, threw the fish away, and washed the taste down with some beer and then broke the bottle on the table. *No problem, Mr. and Mrs. Kodak, just some good clean college fun here.* And I'm thinking, "And this guy went to Stanford?" Of course, Kenny looks a little crazed, with those curly locks, but I'll tell you, I looked at film of his college play and there was no better receiver in the game. He would go up after the ball, and he didn't care who or what hit him. Ronnie Lott, the Niners cornerback, and Dennis Smith, All-Pro with Denver, were both playing in the USC defensive backfield then. They'd double-team Kenny, blasting away, and he'd still come up with the ball. Same thing with Seattle's All-Pro safety, Ken Easley, who played for UCLA. And nobody worked as hard as Margerum to come back after he lost all of 1984 to a terrible knee injury. Kenny was a hurdler and triple jumper in high school, and he wanted to remain a pro, so he pushed rehab as far as possible. It included heavy roadwork on his bike, and plenty of Frisbee play, and it left his left knee stronger than his right. We need him this year and years to come.

Mike Hartenstine is something else. In his 11th year as a Bear, he has a streak of 147 games going, the second-longest in team history, and has been a rock on the end of our line for years. He's humongous, 6'3", 254 pounds, and is a weight training fanatic, working out four hours a day in the off-season. He loves to wear his hair long and sport dark shades. Seems like he shaves about once a year. He sits down next to you, and he's like a loose cannon. You don't know what will happen. You think, if I say anything to this guy, he's gonna kill me. But Mike's one of those lambs in wolf's clothing. He's one of the most well-mannered guys on the club, always working, and he gets the job done. He's also the most respected man on the team, for just those reasons.

Tyrone Keys is another monster. At 6'7", 267 pounds, Tyrone is built along the lines of the Sears Tower. In the weight room, there's a machine called the Stairmaster, and it's based on the principle of climbing stairs. It can be set for different heights and inclines. For example, it has names like the Great Wall of China (four floors), The Colosseum, Rome (eight), Statue of Liberty (34), The Great Pyramids (45), The Gateway Arch in St. Louis (63), Hoover Dam (72). The Sears Tower (110 stories) is second only to the CN Tower in Toronto. Well, now, Tyrone owns that machine. When he first came to the Bears, he was lazy and indifferent, and Buddy was all over him. "This guy doesn't want to work," he'd scream. "He doesn't want to run; he doesn't want to lift weights." Now, it's a 180-degree turnaround. Ty stays late and works out at a health club. You can see his growing determination, his desire to work. And if Hampton or Dent ever goes down, Tyrone is going to prove to be a handful.

Sitting quietly, off by himself, was Brian Cabral, the club's father figure, our conscience. Brian reminds me of Opie on the "Andy Griffith Show," a wholesome, freckle-faced kid who in this case grows up leading bible study groups and speaking to youth organizations. Brian is a member of more charity and youth organizations than any other Bear except maybe Walter. Brian's always giving of himself and at the same time playing on every special team we have—sharing that honor with Danny Rains. Cabral has to be one of the most respected players around, a cornerstone of this club's commitment to excellence.

Two other backup linebackers, Ron Rivera and Cliff Thrift, are very similar sorts, both with tremendous talent, but now at opposite ends of their careers. Ron has been caught a bit in the Buddy/Ditka rift over putting the "Best 11" on the field. Ditka likes Ron's size (6'3", 239 pounds) and instincts, but Ron doesn't have enough experience to break into our lineup. Not yet. He was an All-American at California and a Lombardi finalist, and in many ways he's now a frustrated victim of circumstance. But who is he going to beat out? He knows his time will come. The tough part is waiting for it to get here.

Cliff, on the other hand, is winding down a roller-coaster career. We picked him up from the Chargers this summer, a team for which he started and excelled, but which dropped him when the team decided to keep some younger, faster linebackers. Cliff has also been badly bitten by the injury bug of late—he's suffered knee, hamstring, Achilles injuries, even a torn muscle in his upper arm, one right after another. He's frustrated too, but right now he's healthy and making a big impact on special teams.

I remember the music was getting louder and louder by the minute, Billy Ocean's words filling the locker room with feeling.

The tough were ready to get goin'.

Ditka's pregame speech was fiery and emotionally uplifting. He wanted this one in the worst way. It's funny; he never varies his delivery, so it's easy for us to sense when he's heating up. First he paces, then, as the temperature rises, sweat forms on his face and neck. Finally his face reddens and the words flow. *"We gotta make some war out there today! We've got to play with dedication and purpose on both sides of the ball. This is the one! The one we've waited a whole year for!"* By now, Ditka's face had ripened to beet red. *"It's going to be man-on-man, hand-to-hand combat out there. A war! If you beat the man across from you, we're going to win!"*

And we did, sacking Montana a record seven times, knocking Craig out with an injury in the first quarter, turning four Kevin Butler field goals and two Payton touchdown runs into a resounding 26–10 vindication. McMichael played like a madman, beating All-Pro guard Randy Cross to death, setting up sacks by Wilber and a host of others. At the very end of the game, Ditka took a page out of our postpractice book and inserted Fridge into the backfield, partly, we suspect, as revenge for the time in the 1984 NFL title game when Walsh utilized his huge guard, Guy McIntyre, as an "Angus" blocking back. Fridge gained four yards on two carries, one more than the Niner offense managed in the second half on the ground. As the seconds ticked away, all I could think of was the year before, my screams of "We'll be back, we'll be back." I found myself yelling, "Don't leave, don't leave!" And when the final gun sounded, I sought out Lott, San Francisco's All-Pro corner.

"Ronnie, Ronnie!"

He finally turned around, his face twisted with anger. He sensed a passing. We were carrying the torch now. He asked about Todd. "He'll be all right," I said.

"Well, you guys sure played well today!" he said.

"It just turned out that way," I answered, thinking later what might have happened if Craig had remained in the game. He had gained 42 yards in only four carries and caught another pass for 14. Had he stayed healthy, it would have been played differently. For some reason, this thought took some of the luster off the win.

But I can honestly tell you, nobody else on this plane cares about Craig's injury. The Bears are 6–0, on top of the world, flying home at 33,000 feet on a magic carpet of confidence. The plane was rocking, most everyone drinking wine or beer, McMichael and Walter having a battle of music boxes—rock versus soul. As usual, McMahon and I crossed paths as we cruised up and down the aisle checking out conversations. I guess you could call us the club's designated busybodies; postgame plane rides give us a chance to catch up on everyone else's business.

"Hey, how you doin', man?" Jim said as we stood together in the middle of the party. "Sorry we couldn't move it more, but San Francisco did a great job on defense. But, man, I'm sure glad I didn't have to play against you guys. You'd have had them shut out if I hadn't thrown in that stupid interception. [Carlton Williamson had taken one back on Jim 43 yards for a second-quarter score.]

"No problem, everybody played great today," I said.

"OK, man, you keep doing it on your end, and I'll keep doing it on mine."

When I woke up on Monday, I called Tom. He approved of my play against both Craig and Russ Francis, the 49ers' tough tight end. "A—," he said. Then I found out about Ditka. On the way home from the airport, some state trooper had pulled the coach over for speeding, improper lane usage, and driving under the influence. Some folks thought it was funny. Others, irate fans, had bombarded the cop station with bitter calls. Personally, I was embarrassed for the coach and the team. Drunk driving is one thing—handcuffs quite another. I couldn't help feeling that, while the officer was obviously doing his job, it could have been handled differently. Maybe the guy was out to make a name for himself, I don't know.

Ditka was hurt by the incident, embarrassed, but he wasn't going to let it hurt his team. "The guy was just doing his job," he told us. "It's something I have to live with. We have to go on from here. I'm sorry it happened, but let's not let it get in the way of what we're trying to accomplish."

It won't. Not this week. We're playing the Packers on Monday night. It's my favorite game of the year. It's blood and guts, knock-down, drag-out, may the best man win, all fueled by the historic rivalry between cities and individuals like Lombardi, Halas, Hornung, Sayers, Nitschke, Butkus. Plus, I like many of their players, Jessie Clark especially, who's one of the toughest, most physical backs in the business.

MONDAY, OCTOBER 14, 8:30 A.M.

Ran into special teams coach Steve Kazor early today, looking bleary-eyed from his 4:00 A.M. arrival to grade film before leaving tonight to scout a game. The man's a walking ad for somebody's frequent flyer program, but Steve never complains; not after playing four years of nose tackle in college, then coaching his way up from Emporia College in 1973—where he was the youngest head coach in the country—to Dallas, where he worked with Ditka for three years as a scout. Steve takes great pride in his special teams, to the point of always angling for more firepower on his units. Almost every time he sees me, we have a conversation like this:

"Samurai, need a wedge buster on my kickoff coverage team."

"A wedge *what?*"

"Buster, you know, someone to fly down the field, crack some helmets. You interested?"

"Hey, coach, I got a meeting; see you later."

FRIDAY, OCTOBER 18, 4:30 P.M.

Fridge has been busting his butt, running, lifting weights, coming in early for film study with me, Wilber, and Mike Richardson—who I sense is beginning to see the light. He's watching more and more film, staying later, making the sacrifices necessary to make all-pro. But these 8:00 A.M. film sessions are obviously taking their toll on the Fridge. Today, downstairs in the film room, about 15 minutes into a reel, he lumbered over to the corner, pulled his cap down, and started sawing some serious redwoods. Every so often he'd shake himself awake. "Wha, what are we watching?" he said.

"We got *The Thing versus Godzilla* here, Fridge," I told him. Fridge must have caught that one on "The Late Show" or something. "Huh? Oh, OK." Down went the hat, the eyelids with it.

William's a funny kid. The press generated from his appearance in the San Francisco game is genuinely enjoyed by most members of the team, though there has been a fair amount of head shaking, mostly by Hampton and McMichael. But something's still up. A couple of times at practice this week, Ditka has called Fridge down to the offensive end to run plays out of the backfield.

"Guy's a rookie; he needs to know what's going on down there," grumbled Danimal after Fridge trotted down one time.

"There he goes again," added McMichael.

And when Fridge finally came back, Hampton couldn't resist. "Who is that masked man?" he asked. Everyone cracked up, including the kid with the 1,000-watt smile, gap-toothed and all. But really, when you think about it, where would you hit a 308-pound appliance with balance and considerable athletic skill? I decided to find out. I found Fridge and slowly, five feet in front of him, I scratched an X on the field with my cleats.

"I'll drop you right there." I told him.

Fridge smiled. "I don't think you can do it, Samurai. I don't think you can drop me right there."

Ditka happened by. "What do you think, Coach?" I said. "You don't think if they had one yard to go and I met him in a hole he'd make it, do you?"

Ditka sort of shook his head. You could tell he was thinking along those same lines. "Mike, I think that'd be tough," he said. "Where would you hit him?"

"I'd hit him right in the head."

"I don't know about that," laughed Ditka. "Maybe if you hit him in the legs or something."

"No way, he'd fall all over me, probably break my back."

MONDAY, OCTOBER 21, 11:00 P.M.

Well, tonight Packers' linebacker George Cumby found out what happens. Twice in the first half, down near the goal line, Ditka put out the call for the Fridge to replace Suhey, and both times the kid responded with crushing blocks on Cumby. Both times Walter scored. In the middle of all this, the Fridge leaped over the right guard and scored a TD on his own. The resulting spike had to register 9.0 on the Richter scale. I know the shouts and high fives on the sideline did. "Fridge Fever" had officially begun.

TUESDAY, OCTOBER 22

The phones. All you hear are the phones. The whole world, it seems, wants a piece of the Chicago Bears. Sitting behind the orange and blue wall, in front of the blown-up photos of Bear heroes like Walter, Doug Buffone, and Butkus, receptionist Louise Johnson spent the entire morning saying, "No, Mr. Perry's agent's name is Jim Steiner. He can be reached at . . ." It never ended. Sure, Dallas was America's team, and San Francisco was hot for a while after the Super Bowl win, but all they had was Montana and Clark. Now the Bad News Bears are huffing and puffing, ready to blow your customers away. Walter, McMahon, Fridge, Otis. We are winning, but more importantly, we are doing it with style.

This morning when I walked into the club's offices I spotted a new receptionist, namely Mr. Payton, preparing to play one of his practical jokes on Mike McCaskey. As soon as McCaskey walked in the door, Walter went into his shtick.

"Oh, no, I'm sorry, sir, but Mr. McCaskey, oh, no, it's much too early for him. You might try back around 11:30 or noon. That's when he usually gets in . . . president of the club and all that."

McCaskey couldn't help laughing. Even in silly moments like this, it's impossible to exaggerate what Walter means to our club. In the 23–7 win over the Pack, he'd put in what's become his standard day at the office: 25 carries, 112 yards, two touchdowns. Ironically, the game marked the first time in Walter's 11-year career (1975–85) that the Bears have been over .500 (77–76). He's so tough, he's like the NFL equivalent of a Timex timepiece (takes a licking and keeps on ticking), but at the same time he can be moody and fiercely private (he lists privacy as one of his hobbies in the media guide).

He wants, I feel, to open up and make friends, but he's caught deep in the web of celebrity. He doesn't know whom to trust; when he has trusted people in the past, they haven't come through for him. That's when he gets moody. If you tell Walter you're going to do something, you'd better do it. If not, you won't get asked again.

Walter's very tight with Suhey, probably his best friend on the club, and assistant coach Johnny Roland. While Buddy and I remain more father-son in our feelings, Walter and Johnny have a deeper, more personalized friendship. It stems from Roland's age—he's just 42—and his background: seven years of professional ball as a halfback for St. Louis in the seventies; assistant coach with Dan Devine at Green Bay and Notre Dame; three long years with Vermeil in Philadelphia. He came to Chicago in 1982 after five years of private business in St. Louis. All this experience, on and off the field, tightens his ties to Walter. All week long, particularly early in the week when the offense is learning plays, you'll see them together, Walter asking, "Where do you want me to go on this play? How about on that one?" It's nice to see Walter draw strength from someone, because we all draw so much strength from him.

As a rookie, I idolized Walter. I guess in many ways I still do. When I was drafted, I almost begged him to talk, I found him so intriguing, but he shied away, reluctant to open up to a rookie who might not make it through training camp. I asked him about that one time when the two of us were driving alone to a Pro Bowl practice in Hawaii. The sun was shining, its brilliant light illuminating our conversation.

"You know, Walter," I said, "the more I get to know you, the more I really appreciate you."

Walter turned his head. He knows I've got a reputation for trying to get inside the players' heads.

I don't waste time when I get a player alone. I want to know what makes him tick, what's inside the man. "What makes you say that?" he asked.

"Well, my rookie year, I didn't like you very much because you were so cold. But after a while, after I learned more and more about the game, I saw so many people come and go, I began to realize the only thing we have control of is our own destiny. You seem to have such great control of your life."

When Walter spoke, I knew it was from the heart. "Mike, I've been through so much. Every time you turn around, somebody wants your time. They want you to do this, to do that. Sometimes it gets to you. It's hard to find a friend because you start thinking people want to be your friend because you're Walter Payton. Believe it or not, I liked you very much your rookie year. That's why I didn't talk to you. It hurts when you get close to someone and then they're gone—cut, quitting, or traded. The older you get, the more you'll realize what I'm saying. It's tough to get a balance in this business."

Report card: Williams is blaming me for pass coverage now. This man must be a masochist. "[Lynn] Dickey took advantage of you," Williams said. Me? "The guy completed four passes for 62 yards," I yelled. Williams countered that Lofton had seven for 103. "That's not my responsibility," I reminded him.

"If you're the best in the league, the best that ever was, you're going to have to stop those plays."

I think I'm going to stop making these calls.

FRIDAY, OCTOBER 25

Haven't talked to Buddy for three days. And I'm ready to kill him.

The last big run-in we had was in 1983 when, at a Wednesday walk-through, before practice, Gary

Campbell, Otis, Dent, and McMichael were screwing around. Dent never walks back to the huddle. Me, I want everyone to get into the huddle, to clap hands and get out. I chewed out all four, then went inside. Buddy quickly sat me down. "Samurai," he said, "not all the time will you understand me, but this time you've got to back off." Buddy's passion in life is horses; he owns a horse farm in Kentucky, spending almost all of his free time there. "You know, I've got a few thoroughbreds," he said. "I got one horse that will kick the hell out of me if I get too close on a certain day. Mostly Mondays. I got another horse I can go up to and talk to, and if it feels good, it will eat right out of my hand. I got another horse that doesn't come to me at all. I can't get a reaction out of him. But when it comes time to race, he's the best horse I got. A lot of times, I look at those horses, and you guys are the same way. Sometimes, Mike, let the guys have some fun. Don't jump on them all the time. People are different. Moods change. Don't be so hard on them or yourself."

I remembered that talk today after the Shoe Incident. Because we practice so much in the Lake Forest gym, Buddy is constantly reminding us not to wear black shoes on the floor. White only. Well, this week I wore black bottoms but—and this counts—the black didn't wear off. The next day, in the meeting, Buddy's fuming. "I don't know what's wrong with you guys. I can't understand you. Who had the black shoes on?" Somebody, being a smart ass, said, "Mike did."

"Samurai? That true?"

"Yes, sir."

Then he said something that really hurt. "Samurai, it seems the more I depend on you, the more you let me down."

So, we're on the third day now of not talking. Kim's telling me Buddy didn't mean it, saying he was just trying to show the other guys that I'm no teacher's pet. "It's just like Corky," said Kim when I came home. "Don't even worry about it."

But I do. Sometimes, even after all these years, all the "Fatsos," the 880 run, everything, I still don't understand Buddy. He came up the hard way, just like me, one of seven kids in a poor family that lived on a horse farm in Frederick, Oklahoma. "We didn't have much," Buddy would say. Buddy had enough, however, to play four years of guard at Oklahoma State, to coach professionally in Buffalo, then in college for Vanderbilt and the University of the Pacific before joining Weeb Ewbank's staff in New York in 1968. He knows I'm sensitive, even though I don't say much; I want recognition as much as the next man, but I won't complain like some guys if I don't get a game ball after a first-rate performance. It doesn't bother me. I just have to know myself that I played well. That's what's important. And I rely on Buddy to tell me. But Buddy and I don't communicate verbally very often; at least, we don't express our love for each other openly. It's more of a feeling, an unspoken bond. We've never eaten dinner at each other's homes, and in fact, often rely on our wives, who speak occasionally, to relay our most personal feelings. Like tonight, Kim's telling me, "Call him." And I have to explain again that you don't call your coach. But then she tells me she talked to Joan, Buddy's wife, and one of the first things Joan said was, "Oh, Kim, I'm so sorry. I know Buddy's hurt Mike's feelings. I told him to be nice to Mike."

"Joan told me Buddy said, 'I know he's special, but I can't set him apart,' Kim said later.

"But I'm not out there running my mouth like Otis or Hampton," I said. "Buddy never yells at them. Why is he doggin' me?"

"Because you can take it," said Kim.

SATURDAY, OCTOBER 26

The city has come alive, its hunger for a world championship growing with each win. You can see it in the overwhelming number of requests for personal appearances, speeches, business opportunities that are flooding not only the Bears public relations offices, but our personal phones as well. Actually, I'm happiest for our fans who somehow, in my mind, remain originals, predating the Cubs, real football fans who have an investment in the history of the game, unlike those in Seattle or Denver. And right now, especially when we walk onto Soldier Field, I feel the spirit of George Halas is alive and well in the Windy City. I feel like he never died. Not when you see his likeness day after day in Ditka's coaching, Payton's play, Hampton's hunger to win, or even walking the halls of the building named after him.

Yes, sir, Chicago is Halas Town, a tough, hearty, ethnic stew, full of people who have paid their dues, kept promises, and, like the Bears, want greatness of their own. Chicago strives, it cares, it parties with the best of them, but most of all, it comes through when the chips are down—whether it's helping the needy or digging your neighbor out of the latest snowstorm. Sure, the people running the city government aren't perfect, but like the Bear leaders, Halas, Ditka, Walter, McMahon, and, yes, I guess, me, they keep on truckin', working to get better, to prove to anyone—New York, L.A.—that number one is simply a state of mind.

SUNDAY, OCTOBER 27, CHICAGO 27-MINNESOTA 9

No question about bragging rights today. In a game that spelled the turning point of our season, we trounced the Vikings. We'd been playing good solid defense to this point, nothing spectacular or truly dominating. Not coincidentally, this game marked the birth of the Bermuda Triangle, an emotional force that has evolved among Otis, Wilber, and me. We do so much talking, depend so much on each other, that we formed a pact. So before today's game, in the shadow of our goal, we held hands and formed a triangle, tightening the bond among three men who want to be compared with the great linebacking units of all time. We want to be *the best* of all time. Better than Joe Schmidt, Wayne Walker, and Carl Brettschneider in Detroit; better than Jack Ham, Andy Russell, and Jack Lambert in Pittsburgh. The best. Nothing else matters.

"Hey, man," I said, "we're depending on each other out there today. We've got to put the clamps on Kramer. We have to make everything go. God bless you, Wilber. God bless you, Otis."

"God bless you, Mike," said Wilber.

"God bless you, Mike," said Otis.

"Love you, Otis."

"Love you, Wilber."

"All right," I said. "Let's *go!*"

Kramer never had a chance. Ditka had said before the game that Wilber was about ready to explode, and he did—picking off two passes. Otis ran a deflection back for one touchdown, and Hampton and Perry, playing more and more, got sacks—Fridge's first as a pro. Otis's interception in the third quarter moved us out 20–7, and after the Vikes drove to our one, Wilber cut in front of Darrin Nelson and intercepted a second-and-one pass, vindication for a player intent on proving he belongs. "Mike, we gotta win," Wilber is always telling me. And we are. Our record reads 8–0. We're the only undefeated team left in the National Football League. In celebration, tonight the Rains, Thrifts, and Singletarys slipped off to our customary quiet dinner at one of our favorite local spots. We always eat either Mexican or Italian. Personally, I prefer Mexican, because I can down a couple of my favorite drinks—strawberry daiquiris, virgin, of course.

MONDAY, OCTOBER 28

6:45A.M.

"B+," said Williams.

"What do you mean? This is crazy. What do I have to do? Kramer got zip. We held them to 30 yards rushing."

"OK, A−."

"No, not OK. C'mon, Tom, this is Kramer we're talking about."

"Oh, all right, if you're going to fuss like that. You talked me into an A."

At this point, I'll take it.

9:00 P.M.

Time for me to show I'm not as boring as Kim thinks. Call it Pee-wee Singletary's Big Adventure. The Bears hosted an impromptu Halloween party tonight at Nathan's Hot Dog Shop in Highland Park. Brian Cabral and I had a speaking engagement to make, so we showed up a bit late, only to find a Nathan's employee whispering to us as we entered, "I hope you're with that lady with all the polyester on." She gave me that sad-eyed, 16-year-old, it's-OK-I-understand look. "I *really* hope she doesn't dress like that all the time," she added.

No, lime green skin-tight polyester pants with Kleenex stuffed into certain spots to imitate cellulite is not Kim's normal attire. But I must say, we made a glamorous couple; me in brown print polyester jacket, baseball cap, pants six inches above my shoes, slicked-back hair, 100 ballpoint pens in my breast pocket, trusty calculator. Pee-wee would have been proud. Hee-hee.

The party was a hit, a combination of our 8–0 record and some hot Top 40 tunes, then later fifties and sixties. Debbie and Danny, who arrived as fish and fisherman, stopped the show with some steps out of Arthur Murray. So did Connie Payton, who came dressed as a witch. Walter must have taught her to move—or vice versa. Emery and Leslie Moorehead showed up as a sheik and his slave. Cliff (a waiter at Farrell's Ice Cream Parlor) and Clarice (barmaid) Thrift dressed up, as did Brad "The Lone Ranger" Anderson and his wife, Tonto, I mean Michelle. Brad is a rookie wide receiver from Arizona who loves the outdoors and personifies the all-American-kid. He's not blessed with blazing speed or the world's best hands, but he works. And he's getting better all the time.

Another wide out who showed was Raggedy Andy, aka Brian Baschnagel, the heart and soul of this club for 10 years. Basch had knee surgery the first week of training camp and hasn't been able to get off the injured reserve, even though he's ready to play. So every Sunday he's up in the press box helping the coaches. It's hard on him, but with all the receivers playing well, Brian's been forced to endure the pain of the hardest game in all of sport: the waiting game.

Oh, and Andy Frederick may have found a new career. He came dressed as Freddy, the wacky cult killer from the *Friday the 13th* movies. Pee-wee stayed as far away from Freddy as possible. After all, it was a Halloween party.

Hee-hee.

"I think this team is about to explode. On Tuesday, Richardson popped off in the locker room, saying he'd buy lunch for anyone who knocks another quarterback out of the game. McMichael lost it. 'It's a lot of blanking crap.' he said in the papers. Then Buddy, at a press luncheon, did a number on Ditka and Perry, climaxing the entire show by forgetting Richardson's name."

9
NOVEMBER 1985

SUNDAY, NOVEMBER 3, 10:30 A.M.

I'm sitting in the locker room 90 minutes before today's rematch with the Packers. As usual, I'm half-dressed, wearing my Bears pants and a T-shirt, my Walkman tuned to Teddy Pendergrass belting out "This One's for You." It sure is, Green Bay! I've watched mountains of film this week, tearing apart the tendencies of Green Bay's quarterback Lynn Dickey, who seems to enjoy a particularly good rapport with the referees, and also his backup Jim Zorn, memorizing the patterned routes of Paul Coffman, the Pack's talented tight end. There's a war going on. The Packers are a very proud and extremely physical football team, and they took umbrage at our beating them on national television two weeks ago. In their minds, we rubbed their noses in it when Fridge found paydirt. They're also calling us cheap shots, and after watching the films, I've got to admit, in some cases they've got a point.

147

We weren't exactly Boy Scouts, either, but at least it wasn't premeditated.

Last night in the hotel room, Cliff and I got our minds off this game by lapsing into what is now our weekly, or semiweekly personal discussion about life, family, and the future of the human race. Cliff, as I said, has experienced his fair share of frustrations. "Mike," he said, "I know I had All-Pro ability, I knew I was great, but those injuries came and, boy, it seemed like they all hit at once. And they just kept coming." We're growing closer all the time. At 31, he's already the father of a 10-year-old daughter and a 12-year-old son, has a wonderful wife, and, coming from Oklahoma, lends an old-fashioned flavor to his beliefs.

"Cliff, what kind of father do you think you are?"

"Pretty good, but I've got some faults."

"How do you handle kids?"

"It's a delicate thing, Mike. You have to treat each one differently. Most of the time I try to talk a lot more than I spank."

Talking with Cliff always reminds me of my answer when people ask about my hobbies. "Communicating," I say. "Talking to kids, people, anyone." It may seem strange, but on airplanes, if folks tell me they're divorced (I usually ask about their family life), I ask them what happened. And you know, 90 percent can't tell me. "We just grew apart from each other," they say. "It's really hard to communicate." To me, the lack of personal communication between man and wife, father and son, mother and daughter, country and country, may be our biggest problem. Talk more, I've found, and you'll fight a lot less.

Much of my talk these days is with my nieces and nephews. I'm constantly quizzing the older ones about their values in life because I know they'll act as examples for the younger ones. I always ask who they're dating, what's important to them, do you want to get an education, a job, and if so, what job? What are they doing to help their family? What kind of boy or girl are they dating? Do they like their jobs? Do they get up on time? Would they be a good parent, or spouse?

When I talk to the boys, particularly my nephew Roger, a 6'4", 250-pound freshman linebacker at Nebraska who runs like a deer and has girlfriends out of his ears, I pester them, drilling them about the importance of school, the types of girls they date. Does she have to have a nice car to drive around in? Is she happy just walking around campus? Sometimes they just look at me with a blank stare. I know it's too philosophical at times, but four years from now, the cheers of 100,000 fans are going to fade. Roger can go home, like so many others, and pump gas or be a security guard. But he can also get a degree, take advantage of a free education, and make something of his life.

Of course, against the Packers no amount of talking is going to help. So what we've got here is the makings of a 12-round, knock-down, drag-out, let-the-best-man-win ball game. I love it! Ditka, in his pregame speech, left no doubt what he wanted to see. "Men," he said, starting out slowly, "I'm not going to scream. I'm not going to holler." Then he began to pace. And sweat. And his face turned red. *"You know I really don't like these guys! They've been calling us cheap shots. Low-lifes! This is what they're saying about you!"* Ditka's face is on a full-scale red alert now. *"You know I really don't like these guys! I just want to let you know how I feel!"*

9:00 P.M., Airborne

The feeling turned out to be quite mutual, the muddy field a fitting metaphor for the dirty play exhibited on both sides. The most blatant cheap shot in a day full of thuggery was the hit Ken Stills put on Matt Suhey so long after the first-half play was over that the only whistle you could hear was in the wind. It was totally ridiculous. Matt was standing still when Stills ran over him. It cost the Pack 15 yards, but it could have cost Matt his career. In all 15 penalties were called (seven personal fouls) and another 10 were either declined or offset.

Walter, after being forechecked out of bounds in the first half by Mark Lee, who was ejected, rebounded to ramble for 192 of the sweetest yards of his career, proving once and for all that he's worth every penny of the $240,000 a year the Bears will be paying him for the next 40-odd years. "The greatest exhibition of running football I've ever seen in my life," Ditka gushed after Walter's incredible 27-yard touchdown run in the fourth quarter lifted us to a 16–10 win. The most amazing sight of the day, however, had to be our first score, a four-yard pass from McMahon to—guess who?—William Perry. Once again, Cumby was on the spot. Again he failed. When Fridge went into motion right, the Pack expected another Payton patrol into the end zone. Instead, Fridge sidestepped Cumby and easily grabbed McMahon's floater for six points.

Ken Taylor, subbing for an injured Mike Richardson, had a rough day. Ken's a free agent who made the club out of Oregon State, and he has ideal size for a corner (6'2", 186 pounds) with great speed. But he's not a Bear corner. Not yet. "You're in a Bear huddle now; welcome to the NFL," I told him during the first series. But Kenny wasn't playing like a Bear. He didn't fit. A Bear is physical, smart, aggressive— he'll knock your pilot light out if you give him half a chance. On a couple of sweeps today, far too many, Ken let the runner turn the corner. "Don't let them run by you like that!" I growled. "You've got to hit them! Let's get it going now. C'mon . . ."

I think Ken understood me; I know he understood Buddy. "He missed tackles; he didn't show me anything," Buddy complained later in the week. "We're going to start [rookie Reggie] Phillips. I hope he can do better than the other guy."

Personally, I'm not concerned about our future with either Ken or Reggie at the corners. Ken has Mike Haynes-type skills, if only he'd realize he's got to push himself physically. Reggie, on the other hand, is very cocky, a Gary Green-style player. Still, my favorite phrase is "Let's work," and both rookies have yet to learn the importance of it.

For me, the Green Bay rematch marked one of my best efforts of the year. I had a season-high 12 tackles, helped limit Clark to 58 yards on 17 carries, and held Coffman to just three catches. I also threw my best tantrum of the season when an official ruled a complete pass after I stripped Coffman of the ball. "No, no, no! *No way!*" I screamed, pounding the turf with every word. Then I noticed the penalty flag on the ground; someone said, "It's on you, Samurai." I tore after the official, screaming, "Why me! I didn't curse." The ref just laughed. "I'm trying to keep everything cool around here," he said. "I don't want any problems." Problems? He doesn't consider fifteen penalties problems?

Report Card: Williams says the MVP race is heating up. I'm still pushing Walter, especially since he's run for four straight 100-yard games. But Williams is pushing Marcus Allen of the Raiders. I told him nobody cared about the Raiders; they needed to make the playoffs first. "Marcus is coming on," Tom said. "And what about me?" "A—," said Williams.

THURSDAY, NOVEMBER 7

Came home tonight on Cloud Nine after meeting one Chicago institution and, at the same time, bumping into one of the men I admire most, Dr.

Robert Schuller. Hampton, McCaskey, and I went down to Channel 11 to do "Kup's Show," Irv Kupcinet's talk show. Irv was pleasant, coolly professional, and asked solid questions about players' salaries and drug use, questions befitting his stature as a *Sun-Times* columnist, former NFL player and official, and broadcaster for the Bears. He knew what buttons to push. I just didn't want to respond to them all, particularly the salary issue. Not with McCaskey nearby. No sense throwing salt on old— and still somewhat open—wounds.

The highlight of the night, however, came when I was walking out and met Dr. Schuller, who was on the program to promote his latest book, *The Be (Happy) Attitudes.* It was strange. I felt like a fan, wanting to ask for the book and an autograph. I declined, instead introducing myself and mentioning how much I enjoy his program every Sunday. He thanked me and wished me luck on Sunday against Detroit. "But you know I've got to go with the Rams in the Super Bowl," he said.

"Well, you stick with the Rams, and I'll stick with the Bears," I answered. "But just don't get mad at me when we beat them."

Schuller's teaching resembles that of one of my most inspirational teachers, Dr. Norman Vincent Peale, whose book *The Power of Positive Thinking* is my all-time favorite. Both men stress faith in overcoming adversity, the importance of believing in yourself, the belief that the first step in climbing any mountain is putting that first foot forward. Too many of us sit down and wish. Life isn't about wishing. It's about doing. Peale talks about the freedom to believe, to dream, to look beyond the desperation of the six o'clock news, beyond drug abuse, starvation, and homeless families. He preaches that whatever the situation is, as long as you've got breath, you've got a chance. It's not about talking. Like Peale, I believe there are too many people sitting around finding fault with each other these days. But what are they—you—doing to help, to make this planet a better place to live. I'll always remember this expression and it seems to speak right to our tendency as a nation to complain about our personal plight in life: "It's hard to rock the boat when you're rowing." So pick up a paddle. Fortunately, I'm in a position now where I can reach back and pull someone toward me. And right now, the only way I can do it is the way I act, the way I dress, think, talk, and play.

WEDNESDAY, NOVEMBER 6

Hampton agreed to a new four-year, $2.7-million contract today, and it couldn't happen to a more deserving athlete. Dan's been playing in pain for much of his seven-year career, and this contract will give him, at 28, the security he deserves. Most of the time I'm amazed that Dan's even on the field, though more and more, he's resting his battered knees during the week and becoming a game-day player. Kim told me once how Dan's wife, Terry, has to pull him out of bed most mornings, the pain is so terrible.

I've always found Dan to be a complex person wrapped in rather simple tastes. He loves music and can play six instruments, including sax, piano, and classical guitar. At times, he displays the fragile temperament of a concert performer. That's one thing about Dan: he needs to be told he's good; he requires constant reassurance, whether it be from Buddy, his wife, or his teammates. Maybe that's why, when the season's over, he and Terry hightail it down to the huge farm in Arkansas they just bought. Last year, after the San Francisco playoff game, the players took an earlier charter home than the wives. Dan begged Terry to find a similiar flight so they could get home, pack, and drive straight through to Arkansas. He didn't want to wait one second to get back to nature. And once Dan's there, forget it; he reverts to the country kid he was, growing up in Cabot, Arkansas, before he became an All-American defensive end for the Razorbacks. He just sits up on the tractor and plows his field happily, calling all his cows and pigs by name.

But right now, I hope that farm is the last thing on Dan's mind. We need his leadership, his wildness, on that defensive line, even if he was pushed out to end last week so Perry could start. With Fridge plugging up the middle now, offensive lines can't double-team Hampton, Dent, and Fridge. Somebody has to be open, and it's usually Dent. I know Dan's hurting; playing outside is not what he wants to do—not with those knees. What he gains by missing the constant contact on his knees from the guards and centers inside he loses emotionally by being out of the action. It's a game of "Catch-22," but he'll play it; he always does.

NEWS FLASH (Nov. 8, 1985), CHICAGO: Chicago Bears coach Mike Ditka pleaded not guilty today to driving under the influence of alcohol but was found guilty by a Schaumberg Circuit Court judge, sentenced to one year of court-supervised probation, and fined $300.

NEWS FLASH II: Fridgemania has officially reached mythical proportions. Carson and Letterman have called. Hope's interested, a book's in the works, and every day at practice a new set of scribes arrives, hoping to capture the "real" William Perry. London TV is sending daily dispatches back to Britannia; the Japanese seem keenly interested in the cultural significance of a 308-pound Bear becoming a cult figure. Then again, so are we. Most of us see the spotlight now focused on William as nothing more than providence for him and a much-needed safety valve for us, a way to survive the mounting pressure of remaining undefeated. With William getting 50 percent of the personal-appearance requests and media time, it's easier for us to concentrate on the game at hand. Of course, some guys, Hampton especially, are grumbling about how Walter's legacy is being forever lost in the lunacy surrounding Perry—and it is lunacy. *Omni* magazine recently called to see if the Fridge could pose for their cover. The editors were doing a story on the possibilities of pregnancy in men. Still, I feel sorry for the kid; he wants desperately to break into our inner circle, and, as yet, the doors aren't opening. McMichael and Hampton ride him constantly, but the Fridge keeps smiling and playing better every week. Hey, when you're used to getting $300 an hour to sign autographs, and suddenly your price is $5,000, why frown?

SATURDAY, NOVEMBER 9

Sometimes Jim carries this playing-in-pain business too far. Last year the line almost had to remove him physically from the huddle during the Raiders game after he took a kidney shot and couldn't breathe enough to call signals. I mean, he almost *died.* Right now, you can see his shoulder is aching, he's not practicing, yet still talking about playing on Sunday. I told him today not to go out near the field unless he was ready. "Play hurt and you'll have to answer to me," I said. Jim smiled, laughing it off, but he could tell I wasn't joking. The Lions are certainly no laughing matter; this is a real grudge match. Detroit always plays us tough and, like New England or Minnesota, they pride themselves on an opportunistic defense, creating errors that turn into points that win ball games. Already this year they've upset Dallas, San Francisco, and Miami at home. Granted, we're at Soldier Field this week, but with the we-can-beat-them-hands-down attitude I'm sensing around here, I'm still a little nervous.

Watching film on Detroit didn't help any. Their running back, James Jones, is a bruiser, one of the best and most underrated backs in the league. He'll knock your jock off if you give him half a reason. Their quarterback, Eric Hipple, is no Montana, but he plays with a big heart, can scramble, and has an uncanny ability to make the big play. What makes him human is inconsistency and playing behind an offensive line that's really banged up—the Lions have been forced to shift a lot of folks around. Defensively, you can make adjustments on the line. Not on offense. Still, the Lions remind me of a wounded animal: more dangerous when injured, ready to strike out at anyone to protect their turf.

I've always honestly felt that our defense is our best offense and our offense our best defense. In my mind, our offense's job is to run the clock, keep the other team's offense off the field, and not make stupid turnovers. Our job, meanwhile, is just the opposite—stay off the field, but wreak as much havoc as possible when we do step on. And get the offense the ball in great field position where it can produce points. It's Ditka's dream, but the real brains, the nuts and bolts behind it, is our offensive coordinator, Ed Hughes. Ed is a quiet, unaffected, imperturbable man whose poker face hides a football fire that burns in his body 24 hours a day. A compulsive note-taker, he's invariably scribbling down ideas, formations, or plays as they pop into his head—at all hours of the day or night. Ed's a lifer. The Bears are his 11th team; he worked with Ditka previously in Dallas (1973–76) and served a stint as the head coach of the Houston Oilers. Every week, he breaks down every offensive play by formation, down, distance, and blocking scheme, and gives each man a grade on each play. He loves it, especially later in the week when he gets a chance to insert a trick play or two into the game plan. The Payton-to McMahon touchdown pass we pulled off against the Vikes in week 8 was his idea; so was Fridge's goal-line halfback option pass. And Ed's interested in defensive philosophy, too. He'll ask me about the complexities of the 46, how I would attack it. "If the offensive line really fired out, would it be hard for you guys to get your reads and make your adjustments?" he said one day. I told him yes, in theory, we'd have trouble, but practically, no line is perfect; nobody fires out and shields defenders 100 percent of the time. There would always be one lazy lineman, someone to give it away, and sooner or later I'd find that person on film, the weak link. Then we'd exploit it.

SUNDAY, NOVEMBER 10, 8:00 P.M.

Well, today Ditka's dreams came true as we whipped Detroit 24–3. The offense held the ball for 41:02 minutes, more than two-thirds of the game. And for only the third time in his career, Matt Suhey ran for more than 100 yards (he had 102), while Walter rushed for 107. Our first 21 plays were on the ground, and Fuller, subbing for McMahon, threw only 13 total passes, completing seven. On defense, we chalked up four sacks, two fumble recoveries (thank you very much), and two interceptions in less than 19 minutes. Fridge had a big game, five tackles and two sacks, but the day really belonged to Suhey, who played terrifically in front of a terrific lady—his mother—who had just returned from a three-month visit to Japan.

I love Matt. To me, he's like the Paul Volcker of the

Bears. It might seem a funny analogy, but like Volcker, who chairs the Federal Reserve Board in Washington and directs our nation's money supply, Matt runs interference for Walter and, at the same time, controls the tempo of our running game. Unlike most politicians, Matt doesn't crave publicity, and believe me, when he climbs into his uniform, he's all business. He's like that off the field, too. At Penn State he was a finance major, and he's currently studying for an M.B.A. from Northwestern. But what makes him fit right into our cast of characters is that Matt knows a few of his own. He loves to do He-Man and Master of the Universe impressions. His voice gets low, quite ominous. When he starts repeating *"By the power of Greyskull . . ."*—things like that. I guess as long as he doesn't start pretending he's She-Ra or something, we'll be all right.

TUESDAY, NOVEMBER 12

Finally reached Todd today. The deadline for signing him is about two weeks away, and there's nothing but growing hostility on both sides. I've tried calling him about 10 times, but he seemed to have dropped out of life, never responding to any messages I left at his parents' home.

"Man," I said, when I finally made contact, "I can't believe you haven't returned any of my calls."

"Well," Todd said, "you basically got what you wanted, and that's fine and dandy for you. But I think that how the Bears perceive Mike Singletary and Todd Bell are two different things. I thought my reputation was solid. I made first-team All-Pro last year, but for some reason, the Bears don't think I'm worth it."

It turned out to be a strange conversation. I did a lot of listening, sensing strong resentment on Todd's part about how our contracts were handled. I found myself thinking back to our talks together, to Todd telling me, "Mike, this is my year, this is my year." And it was. He took his mother to the Pro Bowl in Hawaii. That's Todd. Family first. It was also the last time we played together. And right now, it's looking like the last time we'll ever play together.

NEWS FLASH: Headline—"Bears Goliath Survives David." "Late Night with the Fridge and David Letterman." The show and our club may never recover. McMichael and Hampton spent most of the week muttering about their linemate's success, shaking their heads.

"Man, this kid here, he comes in and goes to sleep during film, scores a couple touchdowns, and the next thing you know, he's on national TV," said Steve. Added Hampton: "You know, Mongo, you and I have been here for years, and nobody ever asked us to do 'Letterman.'"

One of the biggest changes you sense in Ditka between '84 and '85 is how he handles the Big Ones. In years past he invariably ranted and raved, hoping to funnel his high-octane emotions into our systems vicariously, believing the more we worked, the more energy we expended on the practice field, the better we would play on Sunday. But this season he's practicing a mysterious form of self-denial, purposely holding his personal emotions in check, concentrating more on game preparation, saving our legs, keeping us relaxed—yet still confident—before games. His new attitude will certainly be tested this week because there's no bigger game than the Dallas Cowboys.

Ditka played and coached for Cowboys coach Tom Landry, and it grates on Iron Mike that we've lost six straight to the Cowboys dating back to 1971.

As our preseason game indicated we were none too pleased about that, either. The game looked like it came straight out of the O.K. Corral. In the first fight (you lost count after awhile) Randy White was punching Bortzy between the bars of his face mask, and then Mark and White got into it. White then ripped off Van Horne's helmet (who was busy exchanging unpleasantries with Too Tall Jones) and used it to bop Bortzy on the head—which, considering the size of Dome's dome, was a pretty safe spot. Naturally, Mark went crazy, which fueled a fight that brought Thayer, Hilgenberg, and Gentry into the action. For a spell, it looked like some Tag Team bout down at the Horizon. Anyway, White got ejected and fined $1,000, and everyone else was hit for $300 apiece. Not bad; heck, $19 tickets down here are going for $250 a pop this week. Still, Ditka's playing his pregame role of peacekeeper. "It's just another game," he keeps saying. "Just another game." Of course, nobody believes a word of it. This is just another game like Rush Street is just another place to go after work to get a drink.

Still, we all know this game represents another fictional turning point in our season. We can either move up, the way we did when we beat San Francisco, or fall back into line with the other Super Bowl contenders. Our game plan is surprisingly thin—just 30 pages—and heavy on standard 3-4 and 5-2 defensive schemes because the Cowboys shift so much. Our motto this week is "under control." We have to be on time and have discipline. We can't allow Dallas to destroy our defensive rhythm. "Play with your minds," Buddy told us. "Don't let them trick you."

Looking at film, it's easy to see why the Cowboys have been an inconsistent club all year. Their Jekyll and Hyde personality is rooted in their long-standing quarterback conflict, the continuing saga of whether Landry should start Danny White or Gary Hogeboom. Hogeboom reminds me so much of McMahon—tough, gutsy, strong of heart. He's also a much better scrambler than White, who tends to get caught in the defensive web. Thankfully, it's White who's on the menu this week, so Buddy's been busy cooking up something he calls the Cheeseburger defense. In it, both Wilber and Otis line up on the same side, outside the tackle. Then they both blitz with one mission in mind: take dead aim at Danny White.

Another obvious concern for me is Tony Dorsett, a running back who, when he first came into the league, I thought was just average. But it turns out Danny Rains played in the same high school back-field with Dorsett and knows a lot about Tony's personal life, how he's overcome so much tragedy— the death of one fiancée, a divorce, IRS trouble, a rumored FBI cocaine investigation. You can't be a dog and come out of all that still in control of your life. And Tony can control a game in much the same manner. Make a mistake, let him get a step on you, and you might as well stop and put six points on the board.

Why do I even talk to Tom Williams? Now he's telling me Cowboy linebacker Gene ("the Hitting Machine") Lockhart is my "heir apparent," like I'm 35 years old and ready for a La-Z-Boy recliner or something. "One shot from the Machine and you'll be history, Singletary," said Williams.

Oh, and don't forget Dorsett. "He's a great cut-back runner," Williams said. "There's no way you'll be able to stop him; you can't keep him under 100." Williams then tossed out some crazy stat: between 42 and 50 of Dorsett's yards every game come up the middle. "He'll never do that to me," I yelled, feeling more and more like the Burt Lancaster character in the movie *Local Hero*, the board chairman who hires a bizarre character to abuse him for psychological reasons. Like Lancaster's tormenter, Williams knows no bounds of mental cruelty.

Williams hung up, but not before I got in the last word: "Dorsett's got to get by Hampton and McMichael first," I cried. "They won't be fooled." Will ya, guys?

Actually, the key to this contest will be the play of the man we call "the Colonel"—Richard Dent. Dave and Wilber are both on a roll, brimming with newfound confidence, but the Colonel seems to be regressing, the contract squabble weighing heavy, hurting his consistency. I talked to him about it.

"You know, whatever you do," I said, "just make sure when you go out there, you don't let the game come to you. If you do, why play? You're wasting your time. Whatever happens, don't let the mental worries wear you out. If you're going to play, let loose. Worry about the money after the season."

SUNDAY, NOVEMBER 17, 9:30 P.M., AIRBORNE

Well, the Colonel came to play. Ditka's pregame speech helped as he took some of the wraps off his choir robe. "We've *never* gotten any respect from Dallas. They never cared for us. They don't know who we are. We have to show them we are worth their respect."

OK. How about Hampton tipping White's first pass, Dent catching it and falling into the end zone for a 7–0 lead? A Butler field goal made it 10–0 before one of my pregame meetings really paid off.

I had called a special meeting among Mike Richardson, Duerson, and myself to discuss a play where a Cowboy wide receiver cuts across the middle and a running back flares out into the vacated area. The wide receiver tries to pick off a linebacker—in this

case, me—leaving the back room to operate. If I step
back to avoid the pick, chances are I'll disrupt
Richardson. So, I told him, "When you see the
receiver cut across the middle, just yell, 'Mike, he's
coming,' and I'll jack him up so he knows he's going
to pay if he comes my way."

Sure enough, the Cowboys called the play, and
Richardson, the man Buddy calls L.A. because Mike
always seemed to perform worst on the West Coast,
was smart enough to smell it out. "Mike, he's coming," he yelled. I turned around and spotted wide
receiver Mike Renfro who immediately stopped. He
wanted no part of the pick now that I knew he was
coming. Dorsett, meanwhile, was backing up, trying
to find room. Too much time. Otis put some big heat
on Hogeboom and pressured him into throwing to
the spot the receiver was supposed to be in. Only
L.A. was standing there, instead. Thirty-six yards
later, Richardson was in the end zone and we were
up 17–0.

After that, we just junked the game plan and kept
blitzing. "Fifty-nine," "fifty-nine," fifty-nine," is all I
heard for a while. That's Otis. He was all over White,
knocking him out twice, making five other tackles.
We smelled blood and went after it. As the score
mounted—17–0, 24–0, 27–0, 30–0—our emotions
took over, football's spontaneous combustion of
violence and verve mixing together in one special
solution. It all spilled out in the third quarter, when
Duerson, then Otis, started barking like a dog. Right,
a dog. "We're the mad dogs!" roared Otis, "Woof!
Woof! Woof!"

Standing next to Buddy, I got pretty fired up. Next
thing I knew, I was barking like a pit bull. Irv Cross,
the CBS analyst, happened to be on the sidelines
near us. "Brent," he said, "I think they're barking
like dogs down here." Pretty soon, all three of us
turned to the crowd and woofed away. In between

barks, I'm eating up this massacre (the score would eventually stop at 44–0). "Don't leave now!" I screamed. "We need witnesses! We need witnesses!"

After the game, Irv stopped me. "What's this barking thing?" he asked. I told him the truth. "It's a fever," I said. "A fever." A fever that helped us clinch our second straight NFC Central Division title, the earliest such win in league history.

MONDAY, NOVEMBER 18

Met Mayor Harold Washington for the first time today. Willie Gault and I went downtown to co-sponsor the "Sharing It" food drive to help feed the needy in Chicago. The mayor thanked us for the 10-gallon hat he said we helped him win from the mayor of Dallas.

I respect the mayor, not so much for the job he's done as for being a hardworking, caring person. I don't follow politics much, only to the point where, like most Chicagoans, I wish the mayor and Cook County Democratic Party chairman Edward Vrdolyak would smoke a little of the peace pipe. I get tired of their bickering.

Anyway, it appears all the help Kim has been giving me on my diction has paid off. Over the last couple of years, she's critiqued every speech I've made for grammar, content, and organization. "People need to have some order," she says. "You know, one-two-three."

I must have impressed the mayor. Maybe it's the evangelist in me. He came over afterward to talk. "Where in the world did you learn to speak like that?" he asked. "You're so articulate, you're so . . ." On it went.

"You should get into politics," said the mayor.

I told him I didn't think I was cut out for the job.

The politics played around Halas Hall are enough for me.

FRIDAY, NOVEMBER 22

"We are the Bears Shufflin' Crew
Shufflin' on down, doin' it for you
We're not here to start no trouble
We're just here to do the Super Bowl Shuffle."

It all started three weeks ago. I was returning from practice, tired, eager to see Kim, when Willie stopped me. "Mike, I'd like to get everybody together to talk to a guy named Dick Meyer," he said. "We've been talking back and forth, and there's the possibility of maybe doing a record."

"What kind of record?" I said.

"You know, something cool, a rap record or something."

"No way, Willie."

I'd had enough. The team was drowning in distractions as it was, and I wanted no part in adding another one. Then Willie explained the bottom line: the record would raise money for the needy. Ah, what the heck. How hard can it be to cut a record? So we drove to Meyer's house, in the pouring rain, me mumbling the entire way over, "Why me?" Turns out Meyer is very creative; he decided to call the record the "Super Bowl Shuffle," and he hand-picked the players he wanted—Walter, me, McMahon, Willie, Otis, Dent, Fencik, Fuller, Perry, and Richardson. L.A. had replaced McMichael, who found the record "premature." McMichael had been Hampton's replacement after Danimal groused about shuffles being "pretentious."

So tonight we all got together at Meyer's, and he handed us our raps. They were all pretty funny, and if you didn't like yours, as Otis didn't, then Meyer just sat down and wrote a new one. It took him about 10 minutes. Willie's was perfect, about running all day and dancing all night. I liked my lines, too. "Give me a chance and I'll rock you good," went one of the lines. "Nobody's messing in my neighborhood."

Unfortunately, I learned playing football is much easier than making a five-minute-and-50-second record. It took us 2½ hours just to get the chorus down. One line. "We are the Bears Shufflin' Crew, Shufflin' on down, Doin' it for you." Two and a half hours!

Otis, "the Big O," as he loves to be called ("sit down," he'd say, "and tell the Big O what's happening"), had the first individual rap. He said he'd show us how the pros do it, having grown up as he no doubt did, singing on street corners in Brownsville. Oh, he showed us all right. Showed us how funny it was to watch one man take 25 takes to say seven lines.

Dent was next. What a riot! The man had no idea how terrible he was. I mean, it took him forever, for-ev-er, to finish.

"Ah, Richard," said one of Meyer's assistants, "could you please try to keep your voice level all the time?"

"Oh, yeah, sure, no problem," Richard said. Then he went right on, doing his rap, letting his voice drift all over the map. The guys in the control booth were doin' a lot of shaking, trying to anticipate what direction Dent was taking.

"Hey, you guys got a problem or something?" Richard asked. "Is your equipment messing up? Want me to add a little more to this?" When Dent finally finished, goodness knows how, yours truly was on stage, as nervous as I was when making my vows. I don't mind telling you I'd rather run through a ringer than remember my lines and sound just like a singer. I think the reason I did it in just one take, was that I was so petrified of making a mistake. If I failed just once, I was going to die, then go on and beat the records set by Dent and some other guy.

Fencik was next. OK, Yalie, the pressure's on. No way was he going to let some bub from Baylor show him up. Right. Gary just tried too hard. One take led to another . . . and another . . . and another, the mistakes highlighted by Gary's high-pitched voice. We cracked up listening to him rap. "I'm Gary here/ And I'm Mr. Clean/They call me the Hit Man/Don't know what they mean."

SATURDAY, NOVEMBER 23, 10:00 P.M.

The record session is over now. We now have to get our minds back on Atlanta, whom we'll meet in less than 24 hours. It's not too hard. One reel of watching Gerald Riggs running and I'm on red alert. This guy is good, a bruising back who just plows through people. Otis is hot off the NFL's Defensive Player of the Week award and Buddy, no fool, is making sure ol' Otis keeps his mind on the job.

"I don't know, Otis," Buddy said during films tonight. "I think you're going to get hurt. That's one big back. Oh, man, look at that. He's just running over people. He's going to run right over you, too."

The words couldn't get out of Otis's mouth fast enough. "Who, who? Me? Not me! He's not running over me. Someone else, maybe, but not me!"

Then Buddy stuck the needle into Hampton over his pending match with Atlanta's great young offensive tackle, Bill Fralik. The kid is impressive; he wasn't just blocking people but dominating them, body-slamming linemen to the turf. It's funny, but Fralik is one of the few tackles—maybe the only one—in the NFL who has quick feet. The rest have almost no lower-body movement; consequently, they get beat on the pass rush so much. But not Fralik.

"Boy, Hampton, I don't know," Buddy said. "You feeling all right this week? You might as well stay in bed. You don't want to meet this guy. He's too tough. I don't think you can handle him."

While Hampton did a slow stew, Buddy went back to berating Otis. Another run. Riggs again, battering his way for another first down. "Oh, I tell you, Otis," Buddy said, "that's one great back. I hope you're not going to let him do that to you."

"He won't be doin' nothin'."

SUNDAY, NOVEMBER 24
11:00 A.M.

Another idle thought: I think this team is about ready to explode. On Tuesday, L.A. had popped off in the locker room, saying he'd buy lunch for anyone who knocks another quarterback out of the game—a direct reference to the job Otis had done on Danny White. I can understand Mike speaking up; I just question his timing. He was tired, but that's no excuse. If you're tired, don't talk. But once you open your mouth, you're fair game. Either way, McMichael lost it. "It's a lot of [blanking] crap," he said in the papers. Then Buddy, at the weekly press luncheon, did a number on Ditka and Perry, and on the team management for not signing Todd or Al, climaxing the entire show by forgetting Mike Richardson's name. I think Ditka suspects we're wound tight, too tight, so prior to the game he went out of his way today to be funny, doing a great Rodney Dangerfield impression. It helped to spice up his regular "The Bears don't get any respect" speech.

"No matter what we do, we're still the Bears,"

Ditka said. "A lot of people don't like the fact we hit hard, we're not fancy, we play in Chicago. Nobody ever gives us any respect [pull of the tie, neck extends à la Dangerfield]. No matter what we do. I think it's time we show them we deserve it."

11:00 P.M.

Believe me, after we laid Atlanta to rest 36–0, I know one player who got some respect. The Big O, Otis "My Man" Wilson had an awesome game—five tackles, two sacks, and a crushing hit on the Falcons' 6'4", 235-pound tight end Cliff Benson that just about put poor Cliff into orbit. "If that ain't the Big Hit award, I don't know what is," yelled Otis as he walked off the field. He had that right.

In the second quarter, right in front of the sign that read "WILLIAM PERRY, DISCOVERER OF THE SOUTH GOAL," our little home appliance did some discovering of his own, scoring his third touchdown of the year, a beautiful two-yard swan dive into the end zone. Perry's NFL offensive career now resembled the perfect ad for the armed forces: he'd scored on land, on sea, and in the air. He came off the field slapping high fives from here 'til Tuesday. "See my sky? See my sky?" That's all he kept saying. It was also good day for another country kid. Henry Waechter, born in Iowa, schooled at Nebraska had a heckuva day.

Henry is so full of heart, a guy who occassionally ends up on the short end of the joke stick because he's so nice and folks figure he can take it. But he's sure got a lot of that farm boy left in him—he loves to work, he never gives up. It paid off today: two tackles, one assist, 2½ sacks and a safety.

Thanks to Henry and others, Atlanta didn't see much of anything, certainly not our side of the field. The Falcons pushed past the 50 only once, compiled

a tidy minus 22 yards passing, and had two interceptions, five sacks, and two fumbles. Other than
that, they managed to get three first downs.

I guess I should be happy that we've now out-
scored our opponents 104–3 in our last three
games—playing without McMahon, who is still out
with that shoulder injury—but I'm not. Riggs ran
for 110 yards against us, even though it took him 30
tries to do it. With the game winding down, Otis was
screaming, "We got a shutout; we got a shutout." I
told him to forget the shutout; I wanted to keep
Riggs under 100 yards. Otis looked at me as if I was
the Unknown Soldier.

"What? We've got a shutout. Who cares about 100
yards?"

"I do. I want a shut out, and I want to stop Riggs."

Now McMichael was getting into the act. "C'mon,
Mike, ease up. We're shutting them out. You can't
want 100 yards, too."

"Yeah, I do."

I don't know, but there's just something special
about turning the faucet all the way off against
great backs. I guess it's the challenge, knowing that
your preparation has paid off. If you stop a drive in
a big game, you know you can produce. Maybe it
has to do with the glamor of the game, I don't know.
Sure, the shutout looks good, but I always visualized
our real power as being what we have together as a
unit—how a group of highly motivated, emotionally
charged athletes can be molded, sculpted, into a
work of art that in the beginning was barely
recognizable.

It was also nice to see our rookie quarterback
from Ohio State, Mike Tomczak, get some real game
action, even in a rout. Mike's a great kid, one of the
few guys on the club who fits into the "cute"
category. We're always kidding around in practice,
as much as I can kid. Mike, who runs the scout plays

against our defense, loves to scramble out of
bounds just before I can nail him. He always laughs,
asking, "Mike, would you have got me?"

"I'd have run you right over, Mike, no problem at
all," I always say. But I'd never do it. This kid has a
definite future around here, as he showed today,
completing two of four passes for 33 yards. He has
a good arm, is a pure passer, but best of all, he's a
leader.

After the game I talked to Bob Verdi, columnist of
the *Chicago Tribune*. I like Bob for reasons that
most Chicagoans do. His columns are funny and
often irreverent, always worth reading. "We're not
satisfied yet," I told Verdi. "If you set your goals as
being the best of all time, the best players of all time,
how can you be satisfied? People are just waiting
for us to hit that slump. People are saying we've got
to have a bad day. But why? Maybe the bottom line
is the only team that can beat the Chicago Bears is
the Chicago Bears."

Boy, I didn't know how right I was.

*"**Ditka:** 'Singletary, get those guys fired up. We're getting our butts embarrassed out here.'*
__Singletary:__ 'Hey, it takes a little time!'
*__Ditka:__ 'We don't have **all night!**'*
__Singletary (voice rising):__ 'Give us a little time! Have a little faith!'
__Ditka:__ '$¢&#¢$&¢®#%!' "

"Hi, Mike, I'm Jerry Green, The Detroit News."
"Mike, got a second? Mike Downey, Los Angeles Times."
"Mike, sorry to bother you; Mike Janofsky, The New York Times."

10
DECEMBER 1985

It never ended. The week before our December 2 Monday night game against Miami, reporters fell from the sky like a seven-inch snow. We were completely covered. They waited for us in our lockers and called our homes; the practice field was staked out like the Democratic National Convention. Everyone wanted answers from a team that hadn't given up a touchdown in its last 13 quarters, was 12–0, and was on its way to immortality. Most of us were fielding 15 to 20 personal appearance requests a day. Eight guys—Ditka, Walter, Fencik, Hampton, Gault, McMahon, Fuller, Wrightman, Tomczak, and Van Horne—had radio shows. Ditka had three TV ads running, Walter was doing a spot for Diet Coke, the Black-n-Blues Brothers were working on a poster of the offensive line for the local Chevy dealers. Fridge? Well, he was beyond belief. Mega-stardom. His fee for a 30-second TV spot had moved up to $25,000, from $5,000 eight weeks earlier. *Need a limo to your appointment, Mr. Perry?* No problem.

The club had also told us they were cutting off most of the personal appearances after December 15, so everyone, it seemed, wanted to strike while the iron was white-hot. And face it: after you've spent years of fighting for the $250 speeches, when someone offers you $2,500 to sign autographs for 30 minutes, or $5,000 to speak to a group of business executives, it's difficult to say no. People want to see us, to hear what we have to say.

Still, it's getting to the Singletarys. Friends, former college acquaintances, friends of friends are calling up, wanting to come to Chicago for a game. *Can you get us some tickets? Would you mind if we stayed at your house?* Between answering calls and fan mail, and working on a cookbook project with Debbie Rains and Lisa Haugen, Jay Hilgenberg's fiancée, Kim is going crazy.

NEWS FLASH: In case you're interested, William Perry's favorite dish is Sweet and Sour Meatballs. (And you thought I'd never tell!)

NEWS FLASH II: Found out this week that Wilber is into interior design. Kim wanted to stop by to take a picture of him for the cookbook, and he panicked. "Oh, no, not today," he said, "the wallpaper guy's coming." Kim told him it was no big deal, that they could go to another room, but Wilber wouldn't hear of it. He wants things just right, the house immaculate. He takes a strong interest in coordinated colors. Of course, he hits like no other interior designer I've ever heard of.

It all bottomed out when some guy called and asked Kim how excited she was about our being 12–0. "Isn't this the most fantastic thing in your life?" he said. Kim said she looked around the house, which had taken on the distinct appearance of a Dresden bomb shelter. She thought about the piles of laundry downstairs. "I felt like saying, 'Well, no, actually, it's kind of rough right now. You see, Mike's been wearing the same underwear for three days because I can't get to the laundry.' "

Kim thinks, short of losing a game, something has to happen to get our defense back to championship form. Otis has been yapping all week, saying things like, "If we play the way we're capable of, we can shut them down. We can shut anyone down." Sometimes Otis does go too far. He and Miami's wide receiver Mark Duper have been attacking each other in print. Otis said he'd break Duper's other leg (a reference to an earlier injury). Duper just told Otis that the Dolphins would kick our butts. Pleasant, isn't it?

Naturally, the whole media circus made for a rough week of film viewing. After going to Halas Hall Monday night at 10:00 P.M. to pick up the game plan Buddy had just finished—the guard had to let me in—it was easy to see what we had to do. Dan Marino is the most dangerous quarterback in the league—maybe not the best all-around, but unquestionably the most explosive, his superior skills greatly complemented by the talents of Mark Clayton and Duper, his elusive, big-play wide receivers, and a big blocking back named Woody Bennett. The game plan was simple: "Buddy," I said on Wednesday, "if he doesn't get outside, there's no way he can beat us. We just have to put the pressure on him, just like San Francisco did in the Super Bowl. We've got to hit him, rough him up, get our hands in his face as much as possible."

The key would be putting pressure up the middle, preventing Marino from stepping up into the pocket or getting around the ends. All week long, Buddy preached the same gospel: "Don't let him get outside the ends. Don't let him get outside the ends."

TUESDAY, DECEMBER 3, 2:00 A.M., AIRBORNE

Well, I've got to give Shula credit. He played us for suckers. He knew with the Pro Bowl balloting so close, some of our guys were itching to make the team. He knew the Bears are a heavy incentive club and that making All-Pro can mean another $5,000 or $10,000 in our pockets. He knew he could get the city of Miami so pumped up it couldn't see straight. All he had to do was talk about the 1972 season, when Miami went 17–0, invite a few living legends of that year—Jim Kiick, Larry Csonka, Nick Buoni- conti, and Bob Kuechenberg—to stop by practice and give his boys some encouragement, and maybe, just maybe, make sure his players shot the breeze with the big bad Bears outside our locker room, just before we were due to dress. When Ditka saw that, he hit the roof.

Well, the game began, and sure enough, Shula sucked us in, showing a huge opening right up the middle, through which we so magnanimously en- tered, only to be swallowed up by converging line- men. "Stay outside!" Buddy screamed. "Stay in your lanes." But instead of staying out, Otis and Dent started pulling some wildcatters on us, taking off after sacks without thinking. They got close, but no cigar. Meanwhile, three times in the first half, Ma- rino slipped outside and completed third and long passes for touchdowns or huge first-down plays. Once it was to Nat Moore for 33 yards and a score. Then it was Moore again for 22 on a third-and-19. Two plays later, Marino hit Duper for 17 yards down to our three. When it was over, Marino was 9–15 for 194 yards and two touchdowns in the first 20 minutes, and we were human again, 31–10.

Humiliation. That's what I felt. I called the de- fense together at halftime. "Look," I said, "it's time for us to make a decision. Either we're going to win or we're going to buy our own ticket home. That's what we're going to do." I looked at Fencik, McMichael, and Leslie. "Is everyone with me?"

"Yeah."

I couldn't help thinking back to the 1984 season, the fourth or fifth game, when we were in the same fix. I had called a meeting and asked Buddy to leave the room. "Look," I'd said. "Before the season I was telling everyone we were going to be the best defensive team in the league. It's not happening. I feel you're making me into a liar. There's no reason for that. We've got too much talent for this. We've got the best at every position." I looked Hampton straight in the eye. "Hampton? Who's better? Dent? Nobody comes off the ball like you do. Otis? They can talk all they want about Lawrence Taylor, but when your mind is made up, there's nobody better. Leslie? They talk about Everson Walls in Dallas, but to me, you've always been the best. But until we make up our minds to go out there and do what we're capable of doing, we're just going to be a bunch of football players who played—but not together. It's a shame, because I'm tired of being second-best. Tired of watching other people play at Christmas. I'm tired of lying to people, making excuses. If we're going to do it, let's do it."

Well, this time we didn't do it, halftime speech or not. Not even McMahon coming off the bench in the second half helped. It was just one of those nights— bad bounces, bad play. But thinking back now, with a little clearer head, it had to be one of the strangest and funniest games of the year. The best laugh involved the Fridge, who finally wised up—sort of— to the mind game Hampton and McMichael had been playing on him all year. In a sense, our linemen work independent of the linebackers and backs; they call their own stunts, have their own methods of getting to the quarterback. Well, ever since

Fridge broke into the lineup, Steve and Dan have been working the stunts so well that Fridge always ends up facing the other team's toughest player. Always. Tonight Fridge finally got tired of fighting a losing battle.

"Wha, what, why do I always have to go against this guy? Why don't you guys take him for a change?" he said, dragging himself back to the huddle. Hampton and Steve never missed a beat. "But Fridge," said McMichael, "you're the key to the whole defense. If you don't take him, the whole system breaks down. It's up to you."

Fridge wasn't quite sure about that one. "Well," he said softly, "oooo-kay, I'll take him. But I'd like to go against someone else for a while."

Later on, Otis tried to dupe Wilber into blitzing. Now you have to realize, the only thing Otis likes better than blitzing is, well, you get the point. "I'm going, I'm going!" are his two favorite words. But tonight, he turned to Wilber and said, "Wilber, you can go this time; it's your turn to blitz."

"What do you mean, Otis?" Wilber is nobody's fool.

"No, you go ahead, your turn."

"No way, Otis, it's your call. You go."

Later I found out why. Bennett was getting some real good shots on the Big O. A couple of times he just snapped Otis's head back with blocks. Otis may love blitzing, but he doesn't like getting blitzed.

Neither do I, so when Ditka started yelling at me tonight to get things going out there, I got a little upset. Some of you may have caught the exchange on national TV. You didn't have to be a lip reader to see we weren't happy. It looked like we were cussing each other, but actually, the conversation went like this:

Ditka: "Singletary, you had better get those guys fired up. We're getting our butts embarrassed out here!"

Singletary: "Hey, it takes a little time!"

Ditka: "We don't have *all night!*"

Singletary (voice rising)*:* "*Give us a little time. Have a little faith!*"

Ditka: "#$@%?&*$@%&!"

I also screamed at wide receiver Dennis McKinnon. Dennis is the team's designated complainer. Of course, if I had to play in his pain, constantly running on aching knees, I'd be pretty upset at the world, too. But he is the kind of guy who, when the tables turn, tends to mouth off, expressing a very negative attitude. I've learned with Dennis it's his way of letting off steam, releasing his anger, but it still qualifies as grade A bitching and moaning. And tonight, I couldn't take it. Somebody dropped a pass tonight, and I heard Dennis yelling, "C'mon, get someone else in there! Catch the ball! He doesn't want it!" Always negative.

"Hey," I said, "we're all out here trying to win. Have a little heart."

Ran into an old friend during the game, Miami center Dwight Stephenson. I caught him coming after me out of the corner of my eye, turning around just in time to get a great shot on him. "Good hit, good hit, Singletary," he said, popping right back up. After the game, he came by to shake hands. "You're getting better and better all the time," he said. Quite a compliment, especially from an All-Pro like Stephenson. Then he smiled. "But I'll guarantee you, I'll get you next time."

Finally, I learned something about Buddy tonight. It was the fourth quarter, the fans waving those crazy white hankies, like it was VJ day or something, but Buddy was still thinking. Just not about this game. He started calling defensive plays. "Run *this*," he said. "Now run *that.*"

"What in the world for?"

"Well,". he said, "the team we're playing next week, it will give them more to look at."

"Next week? What about . . . ?"

"The game's over, Mike, but we can give our next opponent something to worry about. There's no way a team can prepare for our defense in one week looking at all these plays."

Got home from the airport at 5:00 A.M. and called Williams before hitting the sack. Naturally, he blamed me for every one of our Miami vices—Marino scrambling out of the pocket, the third-down rollouts. Great. Just great. Actually, I thought I'd played my best game of the year. Now he's lecturing me on how I missed some minor play, how I should have left my running back and gone over and tackled Marino.

I don't need this, not at 6:00 A.M., not after that funeral ride home. You think Williams cares? "You're a disgrace," he said. "You're all a disgrace. It should have happened earlier; I don't know why it didn't. I told you if you wanted to be MVP you had to have a super game every time you were on national television."

"What do you think, Tom?" My voice was light, hesitant. It was all I could muster.

"I don't know," came the words from Houston. "I just don't know."

Oh, you haven't heard the best news yet. I'd forgotten to tell Kim today's the day we're shooting the Super Bowl video. "I didn't even know there was a video," she said. "Neither did I," I said, "but we're supposed to meet downtown at two o'clock."

Well, 2:00 P.M. came and went, then 3:00, then 4:00. Kim and I were the only ones there, waiting for Willie and the others to show. Seems Willie had a more pressing matter, something to do with getting his hair styled. Anyway, I called Walter, McMahon, Fridge, and Fencik, who wasn't sure he wanted to come, afraid to wear his jersey unless everyone else did. Fuller showed up on crutches; everyone else was on edge, bickering over what the money split would be among the so-called principals and background singers that Willie had invited. It was like a bunch of shoppers haggling over a sale rack. I felt the guys in the back should be paid as much as we were—providing there were any profits. But since the record had already sold some 500,000 copies, we figured some cash would be forthcoming.

By 5:00 P.M. or so, most of the guys had showed. Tyrone, Dennis Gentry, Thomas Sanders, Maury Buford, our punter, Tomczak, Shaun Gayle, Danny, Stefan, punt returner Keith Ortego, linebacker Jim Morrissey. Everybody wanted to be the director. "Turn this way," someone said. Ten seconds later it was "Turn that way." It began to look like another Miami game, only three times longer. So I decided to split some of the guys up, Taylor, Rains, Sanders, and Gayle to one side, Ortego, Frazier, and Morrissey to the other. I tried to teach these guys some rhythm. No luck.

"Leslie, please," I pleaded after watching him grab the mike, do the splits, and pretend to be Chuck Berry all in one motion. "Let's do it one way and get this thing over with." Unfortunately, we found out that for all his machinations, Leslie Frazier has no rhythm. Of course, Thomas Sanders is no Albert Einstein, either. He couldn't remember how to proceed from one step to the next. "Look," I said after about a dozen takes, "Let's go over this *one more time.*"

"No problem, Mike, no problem at all," said Thomas, who proceeded to make the same mistakes again and again. Otis, meanwhile, had been watching Leslie's two left feet, and he just couldn't take it anymore. "Leslie," he yelled, "man, I don't know how you could have ever made kids."

I felt sort of sorry for the Fridge. He's on fire

commercially, but somehow, after watching him do his rap, I felt he'd just like to go home, cuddle up with his wife, Sherry, his daughter, Latavia, and return to normal. I wanted to ask him, "William, what do *you* want?" especially after seeing the kid in Fridge come out.

It happened after his fourth or fifth take. Suddenly William just let go, spinning, dancing, twisting, prancing around like the king of soul or something. The place went wild. But Kim said she looked over at Sherry, and there wasn't an ounce of joy on her face. She's taken over handling all of William's bookings now, and when Kim told me that, all I could think was "Wow, they can't even enjoy times like these anymore. Is this just another appearance, another responsibility?"

Say all you want about Fridgemania, but, money or not, William Perry has paid a price. It wasn't his fault; he didn't have any control over the situation. Sure he can demand things now—limos, first class plane tickets, $15,000 per appearance—but what happens when the fever breaks and the phone stops ringing? "They've missed so much," said Kim, "it's sad." I wasn't quite sure what they had missed, or how sad it was, but after looking at William and listening to Kim, I knew there had to be something missing.

Another idle thought: maybe we can pool our shares of the "Shuffle" profits and buy a new practice facility. Since mid-November we've been busing to Morton, two hours round-trip with traffic. McCaskey says he can't justify spending millions to build an all-weather facility that we'd use only 15 or 20 times a year. Of course, it's only 15 or 20 of the most important days of the year, when we prepare for the playoffs, the postseason, Super Bowls, little things like that. But what can you expect from a team that decides 10 games into an undefeated season that "the concept of cheerleaders has out-lived its time" and unceremoniously drops 38 of the hardest-working girls of all time, some of whom have spent eight years cheering the Bears at Soldier Field? Girls who showed loyalty to our club when fans were pouring beer on Neill, girls who stood out in 38-degrees-below wind-chill weather last year, cheering an absolutely Arctic 20–14 loss to the Packers. But now that we're on a roll, McCaskey decides to put the Honey Bears into permanent hibernation. I'm going to miss them; I can't imagine football without cheerleaders, even pro ball. Seems our fans feel the same way. In some radio poll, the vote was 3–1 to keep them, but the only vote that really counts is McCaskey's, who I think is slowly, *very* slowly, but surely learning what it takes to run a winning football team. He still has a tendency to view us as a part of some continuum, debits to be placed in some plus or minus column. Sometimes I think for all his Ivy League intellect and consider-able charm, he's regressing, moving back in time before Papa Bear was in command. But I can't worry too much about it. I've got to start thinking about Indianapolis. Somebody has to. Everyone in practice is saying things like "Those guys are so terrible, we're going to blow them out." There is one good thing about practice these days: no national reporters. We took care of that problem in Miami. It's just us and the local guys. Just the way I like it.

THURSDAY, DECEMBER 5, 8:30 A.M.

On film, the Colts remind .me of the Tampa Bay Bucs. They're young, big hitters, with a tendency to self-destruct. Buddy, just to make sure he has our attention, is holding a "back to school" special this week. He tested us yesterday, questioning us on formations, down and distance situations. A passing grade was 100 percent, and Buddy is always telling the press that everyone gets 100. Not true. Hartenstine is the sharpest lineman; he always scores perfectly. McMichael is grade A, but somehow I don't think the Fridge and Hampton had perfect scores. It really doesn't matter, though. They do their thing up front; we do ours. It's more important that the linebackers and backs score high.

SUNDAY, DECEMBER 8, 10:00 P.M.

Test or no test, we just didn't have it against Indianapolis. We left the field tied 3–3 at the half, showered by a chorus of boos. I realize fans have the right to boo anytime they want to, but I remember a couple of times at Baylor when the same thing happened, and I stood up in front of pep rallies and said, "You know, you people don't have to go to the games." What I meant was, why come out and boo? Why not come out and realize we're doing the best possible job we can on that day? While it may look like we're half-steppin', we're working. So why not show us that you love us, that you care for us? Maybe we'd play better for you. Don't boo us when times are tough; boost us up. Maybe you're the reason we're playing poorly. When our fans get into the game, other teams realize, hey, there *is* such a thing as Bear Country.

At halftime, Ditka's face was so red it belonged in a firehouse. *"I told you this was a good football team. This club is a lot like we were three years ago. They're hungry. But there's no way in the world this score should be 3–3. If we don't go out there and take the momentum back and turn this game around, we're going to get embarrassed."*

We finally pulled it out, 17–10, but I think Walter,

who ran for 111 yards, his ninth straight 100-plus-yard game, a new league record, summed it up best: "I'm tired," he said.

Of course, one thing that saved us today was Maury Buford. He boomed a couple of beauties that rolled out inside the Indianapolis five-yard line. Like Cliff, Maury is a San Diego castoff who's moved right into our lineup and made a huge difference. He's averaging more than 42 yards per kick, putting us into position to play the field position game we love. Maury's a loner, a polar opposite to our rookie kicker Butler, a Georgia kid who enjoys driving in the fast lane, especially when McMahon's behind the wheel. Maury's just a soft-spoken country boy who takes some serious pride in his profession. We were all proud of him today. He got a game ball.

MONDAY, DECEMBER 9, 9 P.M.

Had my second serious conversation of the season today with Coach Communication. I walked into Ditka's office and asked my favorite question.

"Coach, how am I doing?"

"How do you think you're doing?"

I said, "Well, pretty good."

"Nah, nope," he answered. "When was the last time you really got a great hit like you did on that kid, Sammy Winder last year?"

My blood began to boil. "Did you look at the Indianapolis game? Did you see the way I was hitting people? What do you want?"

He raised his head, looking into my eyes. "Hell, that's not you, Mike. That's somebody else. I'm talking about *you.* You play a certain way. You hit a certain way. Nobody hits like you do."

I tried to explain that I haven't had all that many opportunities. "I got a pretty good shot at [Tony] Nathan at the goal line against Miami," I said. "He got up saying, 'What happened?' after that. Guess you didn't see that."

His voice and eyes softened at the same time. "Mike, what I'm driving at is, are we asking you to do too much?"

"No," I said. "I like the responsibility."

"Well, I just don't want Buddy to put too much responsibility on your shoulders. I want you to be able to hang loose, play the way you're capable of playing. You're doing a helluva job, but I don't want you in a situation where you're trying to do it all."

I told Ditka it's part of my job. In certain situations, I have to fill gaps left by other players. Sometimes I get caught holding the bag. But that's the nature of the 46.

"But that's what I mean. Those guys are going to have to learn something, too. Not just you."

"Don't worry about it," I said. "It's not that bad; I can always handle it. Responsibility is something I could always handle. I'm not going to start complaining now."

"OK," said the coach, "but if it ever gets to the point where you're doing too much, let me know."

WEDNESDAY, DECEMBER 11

God, I love this city. It's really beginning to go bonkers. Maybe it's the Christmas spirit, but more than likely it's the fact that we're 13–1 and the talk of every NFL town, especially this one. I couldn't believe it, but last Friday the Chicago Art Institute put two Bear helmets on the bronzed lions outside the building, and some fans tried to steal one helmet but fumbled it (it weighed 50 pounds), then, 24 hours later, the other was gone. I'm all for the Ten Commandments, but in this case, *I love it!* I feel the same way about fans running onto the field. If you want to come out and touch me, *do it!* This city has taken a backseat for too many years. All we ever talked about at this time of the year was the Rams, Raiders, or 49ers. Personally, I don't care if people paint their houses orange and blue, I say *go for it!* In so many ways I feel like I'm living a dream, a dream where seven-year-old kids show up at school wearing headbands and businessmen wear Bears T-shirts under their three-piece suits and drink coffee from cups with big Cs on them. I dream of people who are sick on Sunday somehow getting better as they watch us play. I imagine kids fantasizing that when Otis or Wilber makes a sack it's them out there on Soldier Field playing before 60,000 fans, their whole week, their life, made better, more meaningful, and we have something to do with it. I feel it's like therapy when we win, and I don't ever want to stop giving treatments.

THURSDAY, DECEMBER 12

Did a McDonald's commercial today and earned a not-so quick $4,000. "It's a good time for the great taste of . . . victory," I sang. Seven of us were promoting something called Playoff Payroll, coupons good for free sandwiches if we keep winning, even though I personally dislike these cattle calls. I'd rather do it alone or with one other guy. We'd have a good take, and someone—I won't mention who—would say, "Hey, you can't see me here in the back. You can't see my face." I just wanted to make the commercial and go home to watch some film.

SATURDAY, DECEMBER 14

It seems the parade of great backs never ends. Wilder, Riggins, Rogers, Dorsett, Riggs, and now, the Jets' Freeman McNeil. I remember McNeil from college, the Hula and Japan bowls, and he was so nonchalant, lounging around, quietly cool. He's an All-Pro now, instinctive, brilliant in open field cuts. This kid, rookie wide receiver Al Toon, is no picnic, either. He reminds me of Otis Taylor—tall and powerful, with great hands and speed. Once again, pressure will be the key. We've got to put the heat on Ken O'Brien, their young quarterback, who's having a sensational year, ranked at the moment as the number one passer in the league, his 24 TDs outweighing, in our minds, his immobility, his league-leading 55 sacks.

24 HOURS LATER, 10:15 P.M.

Normally, we start nine number one draft choices— Walter, McMahon, Covert, Van Horne, Hampton, Perry, Gault, Otis, and Wilber—the most of any team in the league. Today we are down two— Hampton and Wilber—who were excused from the starting lineup for missing too much practice this week. Ditka's penalty wasn't exactly Alcatraz, missing one series, but it was nice to see Cliff and Hartenstine get some credit for the job they've done. Another guy who deserves credit is Bill Tobin, our personnel director. He's been almost singularly responsible for drafting all nine number ones. Bill joined the club back in 1975, days when he and Parmer *were* the Bears' scouting department. Despite McCaskey's efforts, it's only slightly better now. Scouts Don King and Rod Graves were added last year, but it's Tobin who's still picking winners. He's very, very dedicated, extremely businesslike in his approach. (His office looks like something out of the Strategic Air Command. The walls are covered with color-coded charts listing college and pro players.) Bill made a big name for himself as a rugged college running back and kicker, playing for Dan Devine at Missouri, and his "hit first, ask questions later" philosophy has surfaced in his selection of Otis, Wilber, Dent, and Bortzy. Like Ditka, he believes in the "Best 11" theory, and loves what he calls "strikers." "We don't want catchers," he says. Sure, some people thought he was crazy when he pushed us to draft some kid with a 22-inch neck, 50-inch waist, and 350-pound body, but Tobin liked the fact that William Perry also ran a 5.1 40 and was a weight-lifting legend at Clemson. He once told Don Pierson of the *Trib,* "This isn't chemistry. The players just have to think; they don't have to be magna cum laude."

Well, McMahon made Tobin look pretty smart today, playing the cold, frigid conditions at the Meadowlands like an Eskimo. He was 15 of 31 for 251 yards and one touchdown in a brutally physical 19–6 win—the Jets' first loss at home all year. But he and Ditka were at each other's throats again. Evidently, from what I can see, no serious crime will be committed. They haven't talked much since Dallas, but I know Ditka believes in Jim and vice versa. This time, during the first quarter, Jim audibled off a Ditka call, and Walter didn't hear it. Naturally, Walter got his lunch (and dinner). Ditka ranted and raved, and McMahon smartly just walked away. Ditka knows the worst thing you can do is limit Jim. He's the kind of guy who believes the sky's the limit, anything is possible. Both men are cut from the same cloth—hell-raisers, iconoclastic, fearless. They don't talk like player/coach. There's a lot of father/ son in their relationship, too.

The rest of the day was workmanlike; all the backs had trouble getting untracked. Walter carried 28 times for just 53 yards and paid for every inch. McNeil wasn't much better—just 63 on 20 carries. The real star for us today was Butler, who broke a couple of records with four field goals; he's now kicked 28 on the year. Kevin stands as a perfect example of Ditka's toughness, his convictions to go with the best, no matter whom it harms. During the preseason, Ditka cut Bob Thomas, who scored a career-high 101 points last year and became the Bears' all-time leading scorer. Kevin has proved to have the right stuff—a strong leg and an icy temperament.

Somehow, it seemed fitting for a field goal kicker to decide the game. We're not playing poorly; just uninspired. Each week you're trying to find reasons to win—after the Jets, we'd given up only 24 points in the second half in the last 11 games—but listening to the voice inside your head telling you, "You have to win," is getting a little old. The only thing I can do now is say, "Lord, I'm going out there do the best I can. Watch over us, both teams, and let's go from there."

What really made me proud was that the victory gave us a club record 14 wins. It meant a lot to old-fashioned me. Ten, 20 years from now, we'll have a reunion, drinking beers, reliving this year, remembering it as something special. That's what it's all about in life, isn't it? Being remembered. Making a contribution. How will I remember Otis? McMahon? What will they think when they see me? I get so fired up just thinking about what an opportunity we have to carve a place for ourselves in history. I can't sleep at night.

THURSDAY, DECEMBER 19

The NFL announced its Pro Bowl team today. Ditka, customarily, had been grousing about a communist plot against the Bears. "Nobody likes the Bears," he said. "They think we're lucky."

Maybe there is something to this plot theory. Sure, eight of us made it—Duerson, Covert, Hilgenberg, Otis, Walter, Dent, Hampton, and I—but in my mind, Leslie (who leads the team in interceptions), Fencik (team leader in tackles), and McMichael (a team leader, period) should have made it. Everybody but the Fridge is having a Pro Bowl season on defense. Maybe we should hire Remington Steele or somebody to investigate. Maybe McMichael thought so, too, because he and I really went at it in practice today.

"Is Hampton practicing today?" he asked.

"No, his leg's still hurting."

I knew what was next, a carbon copy crusade McMichael takes off on every time Hamps misses a practice. This time, sparks flew when I told Steve to huddle up. He was in the process of one of his famous "Why me?" tirades. I told him to huddle up again. He snailed on over.

"Hey," I told him, "if you don't want to be here, get out; get out of the huddle."

"Just call the play," he snapped.

Now I'm a little bit tight, wanting to finish off the season on a high note. So Buddy calls a blitz, similar to one we ran against Miami earlier in the year. "Just go straight up the gut, and depending on how the tackle blocks, go inside or outside." Well, Steve's not firing out fast enough to break paper, so I accidentally run right up his back. Before I can apologize, he turns around and screams,"Hey! Watch what the hell you're doing."

"Steve, I had a blitz there—"

He said, "I don't want to hear that. Just watch what the hell you're doing."

So we ran the play again, and sure enough, he's moping around and I ran right up his back. Then he went mad, screaming like Mongo and Ming the Merciless combined. I told him, "If we can't sit down and communicate and talk like men, then there's no communication. You want to fight, fine, let's fight. Makes no difference to me. Let's go."

He looked at me. The word came out in a whisper. "Stupid."

I lost it. "Hold the ball," I screamed. "Hold everything. Let's go."

Well, the guys finally calmed me down, and we went on to finish the drill without World War III breaking out. Finally, McMichael came over. "What's wrong with you?" he said.

"Wrong with me? Wrong with me! The worst thing you can do is loud-talk me. I was going to apologize and make some alteration, but you're not going to get anything by loud-talking me. Unless you can talk like a man, then don't talk to me at all."

"All right," he said, "next time I'll do that."

That's one reason I love Steve. He doesn't hold any grudges. Unless, of course, you happen to be a New England Patriot.

SUNDAY, DECEMBER 22, 10:00 P.M.

The Detroit game could be seen as a series of single plays. The first was Wilber's hit on Lion quarterback Joe Ferguson on the third play of the game. Ferguson rolled left, about to pass, when he opened up into a vicious—but to my mind completely legal— tackle by Wilber, who eventually will get fined $2,000 by Rozelle, a cheap shot by the commissioner. (I honestly don't think you'll find a cleaner-hitting team in the league overall. Sure, we'll knock your socks off, but at least we pick you up. And we police ourselves.) Ferguson made the mistake, not Wilber; it was Ferguson who opened up on the pass play running to his exposed side—the side opposite his throwing arm. He gave Wilber the opportunity, and what player wouldn't take it? Wilber even let up a bit on the hit because he sensed the danger. I don't know if I would—or could—have. It was a clean hit. Necessary roughness. That's all there is to it. I mean Rozelle only fined Stills and Mark Lee $500 each for their cheap shots on Suhey and Payton in the Packers game. And those drew flags. Suhey was standing flat-footed when he was wiped out.

The second big play was made by Dennis Gentry, who returned the second-half kickoff 94 yards, fueling an eventual 37–17 romp. After that, McMahon scrambled 14 yards for one TD, Fridge rambled 59 yards to set up another, and my replacement, Ron Rivera, picked up a James Jones fumble (he had been dented by Dent) and became the 21st Bear to score this year.

My injury came at exactly the 13:46 mark in the third quarter, on a short-yardage play in which I got stuck in a pileup, bent low, when Fridge accidentally body-slammed some guy on my left knee. I felt a terrible tear. A guy was on me and I lay helpless, blocking out the pain, praying.

What I'm going to say next may be pretty hard to believe for some of you, but it's true. It's happened once before, in high school, when I was always praying to get a college offer. In the second game of the year, a tight end from Belair wiped my knee out. Later their coach told me they had been trying to get me out of the game. I got hit from behind, near the sidelines. Everybody heard it. "Leave him alone, leave him alone," I can remember Coach Brown screaming. That's exactly what I yelled in the Detroit game as the trainers and Coach Ditka ran on the field. "Just leave me alone, let me lie here awhile," I said.

In high school, the prayer had been: "You know, God, I need to go to college, only You know that. If I can, just let me get up." Suddenly, I felt the leg begin to heal itself, the same tingling sensation I felt on the turf in the Silverdome. "Lord," I said, "whatever it is, hear my prayer. Let me get up, let me get up."

I lay there, waiting, knowing Kim, her parents, and her family were praying. I began to feel my knee respond, the ligaments pulling together. I kept praying. Finally, I got up and walked off the field. Pretty soon I told Buddy, "I'm ready to go; let me go." He took one look at me. "There's no way you're going to play in the game, pardner."

"I don't see how you ever got up," said Coach Ditka. "That guy was so heavy, and he just sat on you."

"But I'm OK now," I said, and that certainly seemed to ease Coach Ditka's mind, because he blasted us after the game. "Too many shuffles," he said. "I'm terrified."

Still, none of us took it too seriously. Not now. We're too busy thinking about something slightly more important: three days off.

MONDAY, DECEMBER 23

I took a joy ride with Ditka today to check out Memorial Stadium's practice facility at the University of Illinois. It has AstroTurf but is covered by a roof, so we'll be insulated from the cold and protected from the probing eyes of the press and scouts. We drove over to a private airport and met Vainisi for a ride to Champaign. Ditka was relaxed, smoking a cigar, getting some perverse sense of satisfaction knowing I wasn't able to open the window because it was freezing outside. It's great to see the coach in moments like this, his guard down, reflective. He's very proud of the team, especially the defense. "Can't lose that edge," he said. "We're playing great, but we have to play better if we want to go to the Super Bowl."

He singled out Wilber and Otis for their leadership and mentioned how Richardson was playing well of late. "What's the toughest thing about coaching?" I asked. "What's the key to it?"

"Why, you ever thought about coaching?" he said, blowing smoke toward the windshield.

I told him yes, I had thought about it, but after talking to former Arizona State and Baltimore Colt head coach Frank Kush, I've decided to stay away. "Coach Kush told me never to get into it because you can't do what you want to do. It's too political now, too much fighting with management."

"Management is just like anything else, any company," said Ditka. "Don't count it out totally."

SATURDAY, DECEMBER 28, SUWANEE, GEORGIA

Finally, we're getting down to business. No more manufacturing emotion. No more distractions. It is playoff time. We're hunkered down here at the Falcon Inn, along Interstate 85, an hour northeast of Atlanta, 30 miles from anything approaching civilization. The hotel is comfortable, with great food and plenty of open space, perfect for my mind-cleansing walks. The locker room has been closed to the media; we're available for only 45 minutes during the week; the rest of the time we're looking for answers to the $64,000 question: the amount of money we'll make if we win all the playoff games and the Super Bowl.

Our playoff game this week is against the New York Giants, and it is truly a tale of two cities. The clubs have met six times previously in the playoffs; one year, 1933, the Bears took home $210.34 each for winning. This time it's $10,000.

Before I left, Tom Williams told me I'd better prepare for two battles—Singletary vs. Lawrence Taylor in round one, followed by Singletary vs. Joe

Morris. "The league defensive player of the year is going to be decided in this game," Williams said. I wasn't so sure; Taylor was playing indifferently amid rumors that he was having off-the-field troubles. Still, Lawrence Taylor had been unanimously selected All-Pro. "He's coming back," said Williams. "He played great against Washington. Did you see what he did to Theismann's leg?"

The entire Giants defense, ranked number two behind ours, posed a problem, particularly to an offense that hadn't totaled 400 yards in a game since Week Eight. And McMahon and McKinnon haven't hooked up for a touchdown pass since that same game, against Minnesota. But I can't worry about our offense, not with Morris and Phil Simms on the field. Morris has run for a club record 1,336 yards and scored 21 TDs during the regular season, adding 141 against the Niners in the wild-card playoff. Williams was all over me about him. "All Morris does is run up the middle," he said. "He's quicker than Wilder."

"He's not running up the middle against me," I replied. "He's not running up the middle on our line, and if he does, I'll be there to meet him. Besides, he's short."

"Yeah, they said you were short when you came up," charged Williams. "You've got to get under him or he's going to drive you back two or three yards every time."

Simms presents another problem. He can play. He'll take a hit and, like Kramer, throws strikes with people in his face. Still, Buddy's drooling over the prospects of this one, his bed at Falcon Inn piled high with paper outlining the 13 fronts and 18 different coverages we're using this week, including the new "Smurf 46." That's when Perry comes out and Shaun Gayle replaces him, allowing Otis, who is split on the opposite side of the line from Wilber, rather than over the tight end, to blitz. This puts Otis in Dent's usual spot, over the weakside tackle, and shifts Dent over to a guard. We want Richard blasting up the middle in this one. Wilber, Dave, and I are going to fake blitzes to keep the backs in, to slow down the Giants' short passing game.

I've been studying film, taking notes on the Giants' passing game all week. A sampling:

"On 6Z, don't let the receiver get underneath you."

"On 1r left flip motion (85), watch draw/33—he gives it away."

"I-watch for reverse."

"On two f1, bk offset—watch the pass."

"When no backs down, watch the draw."

"When both backs step up quickly, watch the screen."

"There's no way they can prepare for all this," said Buddy. "Of course, we've got to be smart enough to execute the coverage."

More good news: the natural grass down here at the Atlanta Falcons' training facility has given McKinnon's and Fencik's legs new life.

Got into another fight today. Normally, I don't like to fight; it's usually completely unnecessary, but sometimes it just can't be prevented. Today was one of those days. I can't key down; I want to play the blasted New Yorkers right now. This time it is Dunsmore, 6'3", 237 pounds, my old sparring partner. Pat has spent much of the last two seasons on injured reserve, so naturally he's somewhat frustrated himself. He's actually a really nice guy, despite his sinister looks—the long hair, mustache, the goatee, and dark sunglasses. Consequently, he looks like he dropped in from another era like a misplaced peace marcher from the sixties. But Pat's got one of the best—if not *the* best—pairs of hands in the game, and he's not afraid to run routes over the middle, which is where I started nailing him every time he ran by—good, solid blows that were making him mad. I could sense I was wrong, so I slowed down, decided not to hit him when suddenly, when I had turned my head, Pat came by and knocked me off balance. I took a swing. He looked at me and said something. The last time we fought, I hit him, he hit me, then I put him into the headlock, yelling, "OK, somebody come get him." This time, after my punch, it turned into something scripted by the World Wrestling Federation, players and coaches jumping in to break things up.

Off the field, Fencik and I have been spending a lot of time together lately. It started earlier this week, on the sidelines, when he groused, "It's ridiculous, two weeks for this game, I feel good, let's play it right now." The old Fencik had finally returned; you could see it in his eyes. Every time I turned around he was following me into the film room, his eyes glued to the screen. The challenge of playing the Giants, and quite possibly the Rams, had lit a fire under our resident entrepreneur. Football was number one now. Forget the restaurants, the newspaper columns, business deals, the swashbuckling image. Doom was headhunting again.

Came back home Friday night, and our reception party at O'Hare included Kim, Clarice Thrift, and Debbie Rains. We all stopped for dinner at a place close to home in Highland Park called the Barbeque Pit. It was a celebration of sorts because for the second straight year, I was named UPI's Defensive Player of the Year. (Dent was second, Taylor third.) I can't help thinking about all the players who might have won it—Richard for sure, Andre Tippett of New England, Joe Klecko of the Jets. I've always believed that whatever award I earn is shared by my teammates. If I miss a tackle, we all miss a tackle, and vice versa. We have that unity, that power, a power untapped by so many teams. Anyway, the place was so deserted that the owner sat down next to us and watched us play—you won't believe this—"The Newlywed Game." Clarice had been watching the show and came prepared with some questions. Things started off tame, with one side asking, "What's your favorite color?" or "How many pilot lights are there in the house?" But soon enough, we got around to the bluer, more personal questions, which was fine with Kim, Danny, Cliff, and Clarice, but total embarrassment to fuddy-duddies like Debbie and me. But then something happened. I'm not sure what (maybe it was the ghost of Pee-wee Herman or something), but I was the one who popped the Big Question. Me, Mr. Goody Two Shoes himself.

"OK," I said, "where was the first time you made whoopee?"

Well, Kim about died. "I can't believe you said that," she laughed later. "I'm so proud. I love it when you do things that aren't 'normal.' It's nice to see the 'bad' side of you once in a while."

Maybe I'm just getting into practice, because the Giants are certainly going to see my "bad" side come Sunday.

"This is it. I'm going to play until I can't breathe or walk anymore. But I don't want to lose it here, not in the tunnel before the game. I want to leave every last drop of me on the field, to walk off saying I did the best I could."

11
JANUARY 1986

SATURDAY, JANUARY 4, 9:00 P.M.

Read the Bible a lot tonight, something I seem to do more and more during the playoffs, seeking strength in big games. There's a very strong Christian base on this team—Ken Taylor, Leslie, Danny, Cliff, Tomczak, Brian Cabral—and it's helped unify us. Tonight I turned first to the book of James, Chapter One, Verse 12: "Blessed is the man who endures trial, for when he has stood the test he will receive the crown of life which has been promised to those who love Him." My leg, the injury, the wear and tear on my body and mind, the distractions, the goals—it's been so very, very trying at times. I thumbed the pages, turning once again to Job, a "blameless and upright man . . . greatest of all in the East," a man who had his faith sorely tested by the Lord, his sheep, oxen, and home destroyed, his seven sons and daughters killed, all in a test of faith. But Job never blamed the Lord for his troubles, not

201

even after his body was afflicted with sores from head to toe. And in the end, the Lord rewarded Job with even greater riches and happiness.

SUNDAY, JANUARY 5, 7:00 P.M.

I believe we rewarded our faithful fans with greater happiness today. Dent played like a madman, helping us limit Morris to 32 yards on 12 carries, sack Simms six times (3½ by Dent, who added 6½ tackles), and shut out the Giants 21–0. They never got started, particularly after McMahon audibled off a sweep to Walter, found Dennis McKinnon between defenders for a 23-yard touchdown, his first of two TD plays. But the biggest and strangest play of the day (season?) had to be the whiffed punt by the Giant's Sean Landetta. I was standing on the sidelines when, suddenly, the crowd roared.

"What happened?" I yelled.

"We just scored on a blocked punt."

"Block? What block? I didn't hear a thing." Turns out Landetta, in the swirling winds of Soldier, had fanned on a punt, and Shaun Gayle swooped in and ran it in for a 6–0 lead. Unbelievable! I couldn't be happier for Shaun, now in his second year out of Ohio State, who's already proving to be a prototype of another OSU grad, Todd Bell. Shaun is a great kid, a throwback to the days of old, when athletes were respected for their intelligence and manners. But the best thing about Shaun is that he's a great listener. That's one of the reasons we selected him last year as the winner of the Brian Piccolo award, given annually to the rookie who best exemplifies the "courage, loyalty, teamwork, dedication, and sense of humor" of the late, great Brian Piccolo, who died of cancer in July 1970 at the age of just 26. "Shaun's like Dave Duerson was a couple of years ago," Buddy told me. "He can do so many things, but he's got to wait his turn like the rest of you did."

Well, Shaun's turn came today. Now, it's time to settle a very old score.

MONDAY, JANUARY 6, 9 P.M.

I've been waiting for this game all year. We'll be playing the Los Angeles Rams for the NFC Championship January 12 at Soldier Field. But I can't forget December 11, 1984, the 11th game of the season. Not now. Not yet. We had held the Ram's Eric Dickerson to 50-odd yards in the first half of a crucial regular-season game and were leading 13–6, only to see the Rams score 23 in the second half, beating us 29–13, as Dickerson racked up 149 yards on 28 carries and two touchdowns. I can still see him in my dreams, the goggles, towel flying. I can't get him out of my mind, and I don't want to. The sickness I felt watching that 1984 game film over and over again on the two nights following the game remains.

Buddy knew right away that this one was something special. We sat down today at the projector, him on one side, me on the other; in a few hours we would bus over to Champaign to settle in for the week. "Buddy," I said, looking him right between the eyes, "we've got to have this one."

"I know, Samurai, I know."

Later I found out that Buddy told Leslie that look was something he'd never seen before. "Boy, Samurai is really fired up this week!" he said.

11:30 P.M.

I can't sleep. I'm running the Rams' playoff victory over Dallas over and over again, watching the powerful, sleek, dominating Dickerson run for a playoff record 248 yards. Then I turn on the '84 game again, getting madder and madder as, for the millionth time, I see myself overplaying virtually everything, losing my angle to the tackle. *Got to slow down, have to stay in position.* In college, I'd pounded on Dickerson like a drum, giving him one great shot after another, and he never flinched. That's what makes him such a great back: his power and presence are one thing, but it's his ability to take pain that sets him apart. My mind races back to 1983, our first meeting since Baylor. In that game, everyone on the sidelines was screaming, "Hit him one time, Singletary. Give him one of your hits!" So I shadowed him; that was the game plan; everywhere he goes, I go. One time I crushed him near the sidelines.

"That's it, that's it! He don't want it anymore."

I pulled off the hit, only to see Dickerson staring me straight in the face. "I got gas all day," he said. "Gas all day." And he did: 40 carries, more than 100 yards, taking everything I dished out ready to return for dessert.

TUESDAY, JANUARY 7
1:00 A.M.

Still can't sleep. I'm driving Cliff crazy, turning pages in my playbook, watching film, turning the TV off and on. I listened to the soundtrack from *Rocky IV* for a while, getting more and more fired up by the song "No Easy Way Out," and there isn't, this week, not against the Rams. But now I'm back at the TV, flipping, flipping, until I stumble onto a cable show about a Los Angeles football team owned by a woman. Great. I watch a few minutes, turn it off, lie in bed visualizing, running game film through my mind.

The Rams are truly a great team, keyed by a huge,

experienced offensive line—the only line on a NFL contender without a weak link. They play so well together, glued by the presence of All-Pro tackle Jackie Slater. Slater is to LA what John Hannah is to New England. The rest of the guys are All-Pros, too, or close to it, and the tight end, David Hill, is bigger than most guards, and he can run. It also doesn't hurt that LA holds better than any other team in the league; I mean, it's hand-to-hand combat out there sometimes.

Tuesday, Wednesday, Thursday, my routine will rarely vary. Kim calls and asks what I'm doing, and I answer, "Watching film." Cowboys-Rams, Rams-Bears '84, a little 1985 Rams-Raiders mixed in. Everyone is putting down their quarterback, Dieter Brock. "He's terrible, he sucks," are the two most oft-heard comments. Not me. I'm worried. I see a quarterback who can throw on the run, scramble, make things happen. "Listen guys, they're in the playoffs, he's their quarterback, he's gotta be doing something right," I keep saying.

Our mood is quiet, contemplative. We were in the same spot last year and let it slip away. The fun and games are over, though you should have seen the faces around press row when Buddy bluntly predicted Dickerson would fumble three times. "He'll lay it on the ground for us," he said. Even McMahon is looking at film. Speaking of Jim, he got a real raw deal this week when the commissioner's office called and complained about his wearing an adidas headband during the Giants game. I don't see the big deal. We're the players; it doesn't take anything away from the game. Why can't he wear a headband if he wants? It's not like he dressed up in another pair of pants or a different helmet. So we make a little extra money for wearing somebody's logo. Big deal. Rozelle sells every inch of the National Football League he can to sponsors. But when the players try to make a buck or two, it's no, hold on guys, we've got to keep the game pure, free of commercialism. Right. Go ahead, Jim, wear it. I'm with you, and so is everyone else on the team.

FRIDAY, JANUARY 10
10 P.M.

I can't take it anymore; my body is about to burst at the seams. The Rams just can't keep their mouths shut. Today, when the weather turned mild, sunny, windless, in the 40s, they show up at practice in shorts and T-shirts, like it was southern California or something. Their defense is spouting off about how they know what it's like to play in the cold, how they're going to stuff us. Their offense is boasting how they'll run inside, take advantage of my aggressiveness. They watch the same films we do. They know I've overrun plays in the past, but we played that '84 game without Hampton or McMichael. They won't find moving those two around so easy this time.

Talked to Tom Williams again tonight. We've been phoning each other all week. "What's Dickerson saying?" I asked for the 20th time. "Well, he's doing a lot of talking," Tom said. "They had him on a Dallas TV show saying, 'We've beaten the Bears before. I've run for 100 yards each time, and I'll do it again.' "

"Let him talk," I said.

Remember how I said that sometimes I just hunger for a big hit? Well, right now, I'm starving.

1:30 A.M.

It's hopeless. All night I've restlessly switched my music from jazz to classical and back to jazz, trying to sharpen up my mind. Right now I'm sitting here looking in the mirror, staring through myself, into the past, into history, into other NFL teams that have been in this situation—so close and yet. . . . And what of the ring. How would it feel on my finger? Kim's pregnant now, due in June, and I want so much to be able to tell my son or daughter, "Do you know you were in your mommy's stomach when we played in . . . ?" I thought about it all. The history. The guys. Coming back to Chicago in 10, 20 years, being remembered as perhaps the greatest team of all time.

The words came out quickly, unexpected. "We can't let this slip away," I said. "I wonder how it will feel to go to the Super Bowl?" There. I said it. For the first time all year, I had talked about the Super Bowl before we'd made it.

No meetings tomorrow until late. I fell back into bed, thinking, drifting. Soon I was asleep.

Bill Murray's been running around the hotel somewhat incognito today, if you consider a superstar comic actor with that face, dressed in a pilot's cap—the kind with ear flaps—and a trench coat disguised. He's bopping around the halls, talking to players, getting fired up like the rest of us. I saw him talking to Walter, then I caught up with him for a quick conversation. "You're a very funny guy," I told him.

"And you're a very good linebacker. Good luck, OK."

Cliff came back tonight with a reconnaissance report from the Rams' hotel. From his years in San Diego, he's got friends or former teammates on the Rams, and he stopped over there to see Tim Fox, Bill Bain, and some others. We were getting ready for the team meeting when Cliff told me: "Mike, I just left the Rams' hotel, and they're saying they're going to beat the crap out of us."

I'm ready to snap, half listening to him. "Defense says they can hold our offense to no points . . . they'll score seven and win . . . talking up a storm . . . Dickerson, *Dickerson* really coolin' out, acting arrogant; I guess that's the best way to describe it. Says they can do whatever they want . . . he can't wait to run against us."

Let's play it right now. Right here. In the lobby of this hotel. I wipe my hand across my forehead. It's covered with sweat.

Ditka doesn't say much in the meeting. "Well, we've reached the point where we were last year. What are we going to do? This is it!"

Game films, special teams. Nobody wants to watch. We split up into units; Buddy speaks first. "We've got a great game plan, but it doesn't mean a thing if we don't execute." Then he walked out. The film is running, but I can't tell you what I saw. Coach Haupt is doing his customary commentary. "Look at those suckers! Look at them holding that guy! Look at Dickerson. He's running all over you! You guys better wrap him up! If you don't, you're going to be in trouble all day."

"Hold it! Hold everything!"

I couldn't take it anymore. I got up, stood in front of the room, and poured my heart out. "You guys have to realize whatever comes down tomorrow, it's gotta be us. *Us!* We're gonna have to do it. I'm not leaving the field tomorrow until it's over. *We've got to make them pay for every yard, every inch!* We all want to go to the Super Bowl, and those guys are ready to take it away from us."

Guys were screaming, fired up. "We're ready to go now. We're ready! Samurai's fired up!"

The sound of a chair smashing against the wall

was the last thing anyone heard at that meeting. Ditka burst into the room to see if anyone got hurt. I don't think so. Not yet.

SUNDAY, JANUARY 12

I could have hit a car head on and not felt a thing. There'll be no pain today, just glory, a release of all the tensions I've bottled up inside me for over a year. *Just be patient. The hit will come. Take your steps, square up, don't overcommit.*

The game plan worked magnificently. Buddy had dreamed up a new twist on the 46, bringing Gary up across center, dropping Dave back, hoping to shut down LA's weakside running attack on the first play. Fencik played close, slashed in, and dropped Dickerson for no gain. Then, after Dickerson swept the left side for six, McMichael smothered a third-and-four call for a one-yard loss. Our turn.

McMahon took us right down the field, scoring on a 16-yard run for a 7–0 lead. Soon it was 10–0 on a 34-yard field goal. Now it's late in the first quarter, 4:26 to go. Rams' ball, third and one on their own 47. I know it's going to be him. The formation tips trap or off-tackle. *The guards are blocking down.* It's going off-tackle . . . Dent closes down, scraping off the interference . . . Dickerson cuts back, off left guard. *BAM!* Oh, what a shot! It was beautiful, orgasmic, a lightning bolt that resulted in a one-yard loss. I screamed.

Quick stat: Eric Dickerson, 17 carries, 46 yards, two fumbles. The man who once claimed to have "gas all day" was suddenly running on empty.

McMahon was a wild man today, completing 16 of 25 passes for 164 yards. He showed up in a headband with "Rozelle" written across the front in black magic marker. I loved it! It was vintage Jim:

intense, screaming at his offensive line, "Get your heads out of your butts." His first touchdown run came courtesy of a great block by Gentry, then he passed to Willie for 22 yards in the third quarter that clinched it and made the score 17–0.

Brock was a basket case by the end of the day, finishing with 10 completions in 31 attempts for just 66 yards passing and one interception. Buddy never let him rest. Fencik one minute, Tyrone Keys, subbing for Fridge, coming off the end, the next. Brock was erratic all day, and he finally coughed up the ball in the fourth quarter after a savage hit from Dent. Wilber sprinted 52 yards with it for the final nail in a 24–0 shutout. But I'll say this for the Rams: they've got class on the field. They'd knock your butt off, then pick you up. But I would have taken that treatment all day. I never wanted this one to end, and neither did the 63,522 fans packed into Soldier Field, cheering wildly as snow fell and the wind whipped in off Lake Michigan and the clock ticked away. Christmas had finally arrived in the Windy City.

You had to cry watching Ditka after the game as layer by layer old Iron Mike finally began to melt. He stood in front of us, smoking a cigar, head down, lifting it only to speak. You knew that inside he was thinking of Papa Bear—that he'd finally repaid an old man's confidence. "I just want to say, you guys have accomplished something special today," coach said. Down went the head again, the feet shuffled. There were tears in his eyes when he spoke again. "There's a poem," he said. "We've gone many miles, but there's more to go before we can sleep. We've got a job to do. We're on a mission. And that mission won't be accomplished until we take care of business in New Orleans. Now, take a few days off, but don't get too relaxed. Remember, we've got the big one coming up."

In the locker room crush, across the room, I saw a famous face. Butkus. He moved slowly through the crowd, hobbled by aching, arthritic knees, drawing closer to my locker. I'd never talked to him before, just admired him from afar. He reached over the crowd and shook my hand and offered congratulations. Later, someone told me a reporter had asked Butkus about my play. "He's the best," Butkus told the reporter. Not really, not yet. Like the Bears, I, too, have miles to go before I can sleep. But hearing it from Butkus made me believe I'm getting closer to my goals.

MONDAY, JANUARY 13, 8 A.M.

We're traveling east, driving to Evart, Michigan, an hour north of Grand Rapids. We have Danny and Debbie Rains and their dog in the car with us, plus Mandy, our Lab, headed for her annual winter retreat with Kim's grandparents who live on a lake.

I'm sore all over, beat up, and my knee killing me. Mentally and physically I don't have a drop of inspiration left. I need to rest, to be left alone, to get away from phone calls, the reporters, the business deals. We stayed overnight at the downtown Chicago Hyatt last night, where they'll remember the name Singletary for quite some time. First Debbie and Danny's dog threw up in the car—an old red sock, I believe—finding Debbie's fur coat with most of it. Then Mandy decided to leave her welcome at the front door of the hotel. She had been sitting patiently while I talked to someone, but the next thing I knew there was a pile . . . well, you get the picture.

It didn't help the trip any that Kim and I have argued the whole way up. She's used to driving in the snow, and I'm nervous Nellie, looking in the mirror, telling her, "Keep your eyes on the road!"

She took only so much of that before saying her piece. Thank goodness the snow and the chicken and dumplings will make the whole trip worthwhile. Her grandma makes the most delicious meals I've ever tasted. All we do is eat for three days.

When we got back, I asked Buddy how I was doing. "What are my chances?" I said. He knew I was talking about the MVP vote.

"I think you got a helluva chance, Mike."

THURSDAY JANUARY 16, CHAMPAIGN, ILLINOIS

Our intrepid public relations director Ken Valdiserri had to do some fancy-footwork today to find a hotel banquet room large enough to accommodate the 180 reporters who showed up. Today we went 12 rounds with the media heavyweights—*The New York Times, Boston Globe, Sports Illustrated*—at the same time, answering queries from all our beat writers and the little papers, too. Even MTV came out to do a feature, and boy, if that didn't fire up some of the rookies. They begged to get on camera. As it was, McMahon, Fridge, me, and a few others put on MTV hats and mugged with the VJs. I don't watch MTV, but I had a good answer when they asked about my favorite video: *When the Going Gets Tough, the Tough Get Going.* After all this celebrity, some reporter, a nice guy, took pity on me. "Where do you get all the energy for this?" he asked. I told him that so many times, fans and the media misconstrue athletes and their attitudes. I want fans to know how I feel about life, on and off the field. I want them to realize I'm a human being, not just No. 50 who likes to crack helmets and scream like a banshee.

We're staying at a hotel-mall complex called the Jumer's Castle Lodge. It's very nice but always

under siege from fans and autograph hounds.
There are guards on our floor; even the elevators
are protected. I decided to venture out once, heading toward the elevator.

"Don't go that way," one of the guards said. "Take
the back stairs; you can sneak into the mall that
way."

So off we went, Shaun, Reggie Phillips, and I. I
wanted to buy a tape, *My Hometown* by Bruce
Springsteen, and we made it into the record shop in
great shape, Shaun and I standing at the racks,
debating the greatest of the jazz greats. Then I
heard the voices from the mall.

"Hey, is that Mike Singletary?"

Well, pretty soon the whole mall was inside the
shop, and we had a great time signing autographs
and talking to the kids. But thank goodness the
security guards arrived, or we'd still be there signing. And, hey, we did have a game to play.

Of course, that's nothing compared to another
game we've been asked to play this week. It's called
"Remember Me?" starring dozens of old "friends"
who call saying, "Remember five years ago when
you said if you ever got to the Super Bowl, you'd get
me tickets? Well, my wife and I would sure like to
go." Sure. We each got 20 tickets, and they were
gone before the ink was dry. I told them I didn't
remember offering any tickets. "Oh," they'd say. "I
guess that's what happens when you get to the big
time. You forget your friends." No, actually, I don't.
I gave a couple to my business partner in Houston
and his wife; two more to Fred Moore, one of my
advisors who runs a sports marketing company
called Special Teams in San Diego; the rest went to
my family. Originally, I was going to sell the tickets,
just keep a select few, skip the hassles of choosing
who goes and who doesn't. But I'm glad I didn't.
Kim took over instead, organizing all the families,

making sure nobody got slighted. It's made my preparation for the game so much easier.

The press conferences are filled more and more with questions about Buddy. Is he really leaving? How will the defense go on without him? It's sad, but for the first time in my life, I'm being truly selfish about someone advancing in the game. I hope it doesn't happen, but I realize it's his dream waiting to come true. He's paid his dues, more than 20 years as an assistant, but I can't bear the thought of playing football without him.

MONDAY, JANUARY 20, 6 P.M. NEW ORLEANS

Got a quick introduction to the NFL version of "Meet the Press" today. It is hard to believe that there are 2,500 accredited journalists here, 1,500 more than the hordes that covered the Reagan-Gorbachev summit in Geneva last November. When Coach Ditka said he, Hampton, McMahon, and I would do the first round of interviews, I said, "Fine, no problem, let's get it over with." Then I walked into this ballroom at the Hilton down here, and I swear, somebody had moved Rush Street south for Super Bowl week. I couldn't handle standing on the stage, behind a podium, so I went into the crowd, sat at a table, and answered questions . . . and more questions . . . and more . . . Only about five in every 50 were good, and some were downright ridiculous.

Stop the presses! Singletary's list of the five dumbest questions (and five silliest answers), live from Super Bowl XX:

Q: Are you excited?

A: Yeah, sort of; we've only worked all year to get here.

Q: Do you think you guys deserve to be here?

A: No, actually, we wanted Tampa Bay to come,

but they were busy, so Commissioner Rozelle asked us to pinch hit.

Q: Are you *really* [emphasis added when the question is dumber than most] going to go out and play the Super Bowl, or do you think you've got the game already won?

A: No, I think we'll pretty much go through the motions on this one.

Q: What do you think about drugs in the NFL?

A: Can't that wait? This is the Super Bowl.

Q: Do you think you're overpaid?

A: No, do you?

After that scene, all I wanted to do was find a projector and run some reels. I've been ready to play this game for 10 days, ever since we got the game plan—relatively short, just 35 pages. I can feel the confidence Buddy has in our defense. The man-to-man matchups in this game just don't favor the Patriots. They need two guys to handle Dent, another two for Otis, who'll be blitzing his head off. And you know Collins isn't going to take Otis on; he'll dive into the turf first. So the numbers game is going against New England.

All day long I was asking guys how they felt. "We're ready to go, ready to go," Hilgenberg said, meaning the offensive line. McMahon's not a happy camper, however, complaining at breakfast he had a sore butt. "Yeah, man, I can't even get my acupuncturist in here. Can you believe it?"

Now, with Jim you don't know whether he's pulling your leg or not. I know that some guy named Shiriasha, a trainer for the Japanese track and field team, has treated guys like Willie Gault, Walter, and Jim on Wednesday at Halas Hall, under the supervision of Fred Caito. But right now, I'm sort of waiting for the punch line.

Finally found that projector. Took it upstairs, fired it up to watch some film, and quickly discovered the buzzard was broken. Now this is a large hotel, and I'm no Magellan when it comes to hotel exploration, so I'm stuck here, alone, in this stupid hotel room without a projector. I end up sitting there having to imagine plays, running them through my mind. I talked to Tom Williams; he's pushing James, not Eason. "Watch James out of the backfield, catching passes," he said. "And keep an eye on that post pattern to the wide out. Don't forget to turn the right way."

Cliff is out, seeing Bourbon Street like most of the team, so it's me, four walls, and my playbook. You can boil all 30 pages down to two words, *Get Eason*. The designated getter will be Dent. There's no way Brian Holloway, their tackle, can handle him; Richard is just too explosive off the ball. I put the playbook down, checked out the television, ordered the first of my record 12 bacon, lettuce, and tomato sandwiches. I turn to the New Testament, seeking out Ephesians, where the apostle Paul writes, "Cast your bread upon the water and after many days it will come back to you." In other words, what goes around, comes around. Couldn't be more appropriate with us rematched against the Patriots, who have upset the Raiders and Miami on the road in the playoffs to get to the Super Bowl.

TUESDAY AND WEDNESDAY, JANUARY 21-22

Practice has been a farce. McMahon is cutting an unprecedented swath through Bourbon Street. All I heard about his Monday night escapades were the words *Hawaiian Tropic suntan lotion*, *publicity photos*, and *breasts*. I stopped listening. Ditka was so upset about Jim's cruising in at around 4:00 A.M. that he threatened to fine Becker, McMahon's roommate, $1,000 if he couldn't control the situation.

But that was nothing compared to Tuesday. McMahon had forced McCaskey's hand on the acupuncture issue, so after Shiriasha did his thing, everyone wanted to know how Jim *really* felt. So, at practice, he showed them. Some helicopter was hovering around the practice field like Sky King, a minicammed reporter hanging out the door. Jim just dropped his drawers and showed the world his better half. I couldn't believe it! To top it off, McMichael, Hampton, and Otis were doing a terrific impression of the Three Stooges, goofing off, not listening to me. When Otis isn't screwing around, he's playing Joe Namath '86, predicting we'll shut out the Pats. Wonderful.

"Wait, fellas," I said, "just one more week. One more week, and you can do whatever you want to."

"Yeah, man," Otis said, "just one more week. He's right."

Cliff picked up a bad cold on Wednesday, so I moved out, into room 511, and I couldn't be happier. Nothing against Cliff, but I love the solitude. After practice, around 4:00 P.M., I tore all the sheets off the extra bed, dumped the mattress on the floor, pulled some pictures off the walls, and draped the sheet over the propped-up frames. It made a nice movie screen, and I sat for hours running film, breaking only to order my standard meal—a BLT (wheat toast, mayonnaise, and a pickle, please), a bowl of clam chowder, milk, and plenty of apple juice, at least four or five glasses. Twenty minutes later I'd hear the knock on the door.

"Room service. Room service."

"Just leave it," I yelled. Soon enough I'd pad over to the door, pick up the tray, and return to the films. Over and over I ran the reels, driven by the fear that I would miss something, anything, a tendency, some weakness we could exploit. It was easy to see the Pats were essentially the same offensive team, running the same plays. The only difference: the return of guard John Hannah to their lineup. Eason looked as predictable and vulnerable as ever. Collins and James hadn't changed one bit.

No, the difference was on defense. That's why New England was in the Super Bowl. The Pats' head coach Raymond Berry, a Hall of Fame wide receiver with the Baltimore Colts, was proving particularly efficient in marshaling his team's considerable defensive talent into a cohesive, ball-hawking unit. The Pats were always after the ball, pulling, tugging, holding the back up while another teammate tried to strip the ball free. It was unbelievable. And they were physical, guys like Andre Tippett, Ronnie Lippett, James Blackmon, athletes unlike any I'd seen in a while. It worried me. I knew New England wasn't going to score much on our defense; what bothered me was the turnover factor—the Pats putting points on the board because of our offensive mistakes.

So every time I could, before, after, and during practice, I'd speak my piece. "How do you feel, ready to go, ready to go?" I asked McMahon, then Hilgenberg and Jimbo. The answer was always yes, not often spoken but conveyed through guys constantly grasping hands, touching shoulders, allowing their intensity to run from one system to another.

After practice on Wednesday I returned to find Walter and Matt in full swing. They were rooming next door to me, and whenever practice was finished, Walter would fire up the music box, throw open his hotel door, and start jamming. You could hear the two of them next door, dancing, wrestling, acting like a couple of 12-year-olds.

"Shut up," I yelled. "I'm watching film."

"I love you," Walter shouted. "C'mon, Samurai, let's jam."

"Shut up."

"I'm the Master of the Universe," yelled Suhey, sounding very much like He-Man.

"Be quiet."

"I am He-Man, Master of the Universe, and you must obey me."

Well, after a while things quieted down and I slipped on some orchestra music. A special fan from Chicago had read in some article that I enjoyed classical music, and sure enough about a dozen classical tapes arrived at the hotel. They fit my mood to perfection, particularly today, the upbeat sound of the strings and drums, calming my nerves, which by now were keeping me up late, well past midnight. My mind was always racing: *it's taken us so long to get here. I know we're going to be back, but the first time, whether it's being in love, a kiss, your first born, is always special. Don't let it slip away.*

THURSDAY, JANUARY 23

Problems. The papers are rife with reports that last night McMahon insulted the entire city of New Orleans, calling their women "sluts" and its people "ignorant." Outside the hotel, women's groups are picketing; the hotel received both bomb and death threats. All because some irresponsible TV reporter decided to report some fiction as fact.

It's hard to get a handle on Jim sometimes. We're really not close. Most of what I know about him personally comes from Kim's conversations with Jim's wife, Nancy, so for purposes of official clarification of one man's image, I'll pass it along. "All she sees is Jim at home, playing with Ashley and Sean,"

Kim told me. "That's what he loves to do. He doesn't give a lick about his image. 'Get me home or to the golf course.' If it's not one, it's the other. I tried to find out if it was an act, but, in talking to Nancy, she said she believes that's just how Jim is. He's just rambunctious; he has a short attention span. I think if he had a dream, it would be to be alone, with his family, living on his own golf course, playing every day. He can do anything he wants, but the question is, will people let him? If they do, he couldn't be happier."

Well, Jim was none too happy this morning, holding off meeting the press, which gave me a chance to go one on 2,500. Suddenly, someone yelled, "McMahon's here," and the place emptied so fast, into another room, that you thought it was a fire drill or something. Good thing the *Chicago Tribune* has 27 reporters and editors here (they lead, unofficially, over the *Boston Globe*'s 23 and the *Sun-Times*'s 22). Some guys did stick around to listen to me.

Before practice I cornered Ditka. He's been snapping at players all week, reverting back to his '84 form. "Mike, several guys are doing a lot more talking than working," he said. "We came here to play a game. Some of you have never been here before; some of you will never be here again. And I think it's real stupid to work so hard to get to this point in our life, to play the ultimate game, and not fulfill the expectation we have."

He ran us hard after practice, training-camp hard. "It bothers me, Mike, that some guys are short-timing it. You know it bothers me when I see healthy guys do that. I won't stand for it. It's important that, the way we're playing this game defensively, not only everyone knows where they're at, but they can get there."

NEWS FLASH: Danny finally convinced me to venture out of my room. "Mike, you've got to see Bourbon Street at least once while you're here."

"Well, all right."

We ate a nice, quiet dinner, then decided to check out the McMadness. We strolled around for about 15 minutes, the mob scene uncontrolled, too much to take. "Danny, I've seen enough," I said. We hopped a cab back to the hotel. I wanted to watch some film.

SUPER BOWL SUNDAY, JANUARY 26
9:10 A.M.

This is it. I'm going to play until I can't breathe or walk anymore. That's all there is to it. Rising from my bed, I walked to the window, oblivious to the weather, turning instead to the heavens. Thank you, God, I said, for choosing me to be in this situation, for all the great things that have happened this year, for putting us into a position of being able to say in 10 or 20 years that we were the best.

The bus left at 9:00 A.M. for the short ride to the Superdome. The only sounds are coming from Walter's box. Sitting next to Wilber, I'm thinking how close we've grown over the year, how much he reminds me of my nephew, Roger. Ditka doesn't say a word, sensing, I feel, the team's tightness. We're not intimidated, not by any stretch of the imagination, just acutely aware of the social significance of a game played before 100 million TV viewers, how tiny mistakes are magnified. None of us want to do anything that leads to public humiliation.

2:00 P.M., Locker Room

You can hear a pin drop. My eyes travel to Mongo,

who is slowly, intently, taping his wrists, his shoes, and finally, in this pregame ritual, every one of his fingers. Hampton's got tape everywhere, preparing for battle. Across the room, Van Horne has that familiar grin, that "You got a problem?" look on his face. Thayer sits alone, shaking his head. You can almost hear his thoughts. *No mistakes. No mistakes.*

Suddenly Wilber starts getting fired up. "Man, I'm ready to go, ready to go," he says. He can't wait for the bell to ring. Dent just stares Wilber's way, leaning back into his locker, legs and arms crossed, waiting.

As the game draws near, emotions explode. Otis is so fired up, so happy the long ride from Brownsville is over, he can't talk. No matter. The tears in his eyes say everything. Cliff, on the other hand, sits silently on a bench, looking like he's already played a half. Sweat is pouring off his face, his shirt soaked to the skin. All you can hear is the sound of deep, labored breathing. "Mike," he had told me earlier in the week, "I'm going to make that first lick on the kickoff." Well, now he's so fired up everyone is staring at him. Even Ditka takes notice. He walks by, cigar in mouth, chomping on the end. "Better save that, son," he says. "Better save that."

Countdown to kickoff. In warm-ups everyone is fired up. "Let's go. Let's go," I yell. Ditka strolls the lines, working his gum overtime, getting his game face on. He wants this one so badly, you sense he hopes he hasn't overprepared us yet, at the same time, hasn't missed anything. It's a fine line, and unfortunately, it's us, not him, on the tightrope.

"All right," he yelled. "Let's get fired up out here. This is it. They're playing *the Bears.*"

Standing inside the tunnel right before the game began, chaos broke out. The Big O was on fire. "Let's go get them; let's kill the $#**&%$$%," he said.

McMichael was growling, Hampton answering in some foreign tongue. Fridge was out of control, jumping up and down, smacking high fives with Dent, Otis, and McMahon.

"Let's go. Let's do it."

Me? I'm trying to stay calm, to keep it all inside. I don't want to lose it here, not in the tunnel before the game. I want to leave every last drop of me on the field, to walk off saying I did the best I could.

Kickoff

Boy, did Cliff ever deliver.

He blasted some poor soul on the kickoff return, and after the Patriots recovered Walter's fumble on the second play of the game it was our turn. The first two Patriot plays, my eyes were locked onto Eason's, checking his nerves. Otis and Dent have been given the green light, and we want pressure up the middle from Hampton, Fridge, and Mongo. I'm also on the lookout for drops to Collins or James; if they stay, fine; if not, it means one of us—Wilber or me—is blitzing.

The game plan worked to perfection. The Patriots came out throwing, the first pass to tight end Lin Dawson, who was open along the sideline, the pass slipping off his fingers, just before he tore up a knee on the turf. The next pass went over the middle, to Stanley Morgan. We were in "Willie" at the time: when the back flared, Wilber went with him and I dropped deep to give Leslie inside help. Morgan ran a deep post pattern down to the goal line; I didn't know if I would make it. I spun around—the right way this time, thanks to Williams's Monday evening quarterbacking—and got a hand in Morgan's face. He dropped the pass near the goal. "Thank you," I whispered.

The next play was an incomplete pass into the end zone so the Pats settled for a 36-yard field goal. The next time they had the ball, after we tied the score 3–3 (a 28-yard Butler field goal) we shut everything down. Eason began to panic, losing his cool. The pressure kept building, Otis, then Dent, then Dent again, one shot after another.

It's over. Bears 46, Patriots 10. We set records for most points, biggest margin of victory (36 points), and most sacks (seven), fewest total rushing yards allowed (seven). I picked up a couple of fumbles, along with a great taste of what George Cumby had for dinner in Green Bay. Sometime in the second half on a crossing pattern, I got wiped out from behind by the Fridge. I mean, it was lights out. But I came back; I had to. We were having too much fun.

Dent won the MVP award, but personally, I honestly felt he and Jim should have shared it. Not to take anything away from Richard, who had a great game, but once again, Jim was a catalyst, 12-20-256 yards passing and two rushing touchdowns. Right after the game I found Cliff and hugged him tight, cementing a bond that had been growing between us during the season. He told me on that kickoff hit he'd dislocated the clavicular joint near his sternum. But even with a knot the size of your fist in his chest, Cliff played on. He'd waited too long, felt the stinging loss in two AFC championship games when he played with San Diego, to sit idle on the sidelines.

Buddy had tears in his eyes when we carried him in. "You can't go anywhere unless you take us with you," someone shouted. Another voice: "You can't leave because we'll be looking for you."

Finally, we were swallowed up in a sea of celebration. I sought out Buddy, found him alone, undressing, in the security of the coaches' room. I couldn't speak; what could I say? So I stuck out my hand.

"Bullshit on that," Buddy said. We reached for each other at the same instant, locked in a hug intended to last forever. I found the words first. "I just want you to know that I love you from the bottom of my heart," I said.

"And I love you, too, Samurai, from the bottom of my heart."

" 'Hi,' said the voice on our answering machine. 'Just called to see how you're doing.' Good question, Buddy. I miss you more than I can say, but as yet, I can't pick up the phone."

*"It's going to be tough to win the Super Bowl
again. You don't lose a person of the quality of a
coach like Buddy Ryan who had the relationship
he did with his players and not feel it. The thing
I'll try to relate to them all during training camp is
the challenge. We can fall back to the pack like
everyone else who won a Super Bowl. Or we can
stand above it. We can dare to be different and see
what happens. I think that's what they'll respond
to. The challenge."* —Mike Ditka

12
EPILOGUE

Pain plays so many games. There was the pain of
missing the victory celebration in Chicago, thanking
the 500,000 fans who filled downtown, oblivious to
the 31-below wind chill factor, warmed by the
thoughts of this city's first championship in 23
years. Then there was the pain in my mouth, the loss
of two wisdom teeth, pulled by a dentist in Hawaii
as I waited to play in the Pro Bowl. But nothing
compared to the pain of answering the phone this
morning, a reporter on the line asking the question
I never wanted to hear.

"What do you think about Buddy leaving?"

"Buddy? Leaving? Where?"

"He just signed a five-year contract to coach the
Philadelphia Eagles," the reporter said.

"I really don't know what to say."

For the first time in a long time, I felt alone, so
alone, selfishly wondering why all good people, your
best friends, aren't around anymore. First Grady.

Then Todd. And now Buddy. My heart wouldn't stop pounding. Somehow, something good will come of this. But right now, I really don't know what it is.

"Hi," said the voice on our answering machine tape. "Just called to see how you're doing." Good question, Buddy. I miss you more than I can say; I want to call, but as yet I can't pick up the phone. I see where Coach Haupt and Coach Plumb have joined you in Philly, and that's sad, too. I'll miss them both. "From now on," I told Kim, "I'm just going to do my job and come home."

Met Vince Tobin, our new defensive coordinator, today. I like both the man and his philosophy; he realizes he can't go out and unplug the 46, but he wants to change, to incorporate other defenses, other players, into our system. Maybe we'll play the 46; it may go under a different name. Vince seems to be a lot like Buddy—flexible, willing to listen, not locked into his own beliefs.

Another message, same Okie voice. "Samurai, I just wanted to tell you, you had a helluva season. I'm really proud of how you did, how you played in the Pro Bowl."

Another call. This time it was me, phoning Todd, giving him one last try. I left a message, and, sure enough, he called back. He was feeling empty, sorry for himself. "Todd, you don't know what it's like to lose two brothers." The call lasted 2½ hours, evolving into a catharsis for both of us. "I'll play again," he said, "but I don't think it will be in Chicago."

Had a meeting with Dick Meyer. We still haven't been paid a penny from the *Super Bowl Shuffle*, audio or video, despite sales of more than 500,000 records and 100,000 videos. "Well, we've got expenses and everything," Meyer said. All I hope is that our efforts really go to feeding the needy and not enriching the greedy.

Tom Williams checked in with my Super Bowl grade: "A—. You missed a couple of plays," he said. We talked about Marcus Allen's winning the NFL MVP award. Later I found out Williams had been baiting me all year, making up mistakes just to keep me motivated. He never expected me to get downfield for pass coverage against New England or to make tackles on Marino. "I used to treat Buck Buchanan, the great Kansas City defensive end, the same way," Tom said. "The only way to rile you up was to make things up, talk about someone else being great. But at least you didn't cry like Buck did."

Had a nice long talk with Leslie today, who seems to be on the mend both physically and mentally after suffering a severe knee injury during a punt return in the Super Bowl. The original prognosis was that Leslie would miss the entire 1986 season, but don't count on it. We went together to a revival in Phoenix, and hundreds of people were praying for his recovery, which, at this point, is well ahead of schedule. Don't be surprised if Leslie is in a Bear uniform, and on the field, well before the end of '86.

Same with Dennis McKinnon, who's also recovering from knee surgery. Say what you want about Dennis's attitude at times (and I have), but when he puts his mind to something there's no stopping him. He wants to play, not just in '86 but in years beyond. He wants to prove to the public what most cornerbacks around the league already know: Dennis is one of the best wide receivers in the business— underrated, yes, but as dangerous as they come.

My father has divorced again, moving closer to

the new dream house we're building for my mom. He's even considering a return to the ministry. They're best friends now, closer than they ever were when married. I realize now that both my mom and dad had their faults. It's a shame two people who spent 35 years together, through good times and bad, who raised 10 kids, had to suffer so much. Who knows? Maybe there's a happy ending there somewhere. Either way, I'll always love both of them.

Where am I? How am I doing? How do I rate? Ditka told me I could go down as the greatest, maybe the greatest Bear linebacker, he's not quite sure yet. I definitely have my goals for 1986: I want the MVP award more than ever, to move one step closer to being the best linebacker who ever played. To that end, I started my own two-a-days the first of June, lifting weights in my own private gym (the basement of a local union hall), running the hill, swimming, driven to be stronger, faster, leaner and meaner than ever before. But more important than any personal goals, I want to continue to be a part of a team that is remembered as extraordinary, that left no stone unturned, a team that motivated a city, its fans; not a team that played and won, but a team that reached out to other people, that raised money for charity. And I want to continue to work to change the image of the dumb jock, to leave the game prepared to make as much of a difference in board rooms as I did in the locker room. To change the image of the athlete as one who ends up working on a garbage truck, or selling drugs, and to inform the fans that we're human. Yes, we make mistakes. But don't compound our errors by habitually scrutinizing our lives or putting us on pedestals. If we miss a tackle or throw an interception, help us back, show us you care. Don't be afraid to

stand up and speak up. Dare to be different. Finally,
I guess in the end, I want to make the name Singletary something special. To have it remembered, like
the 1985 Chicago Bears season, a year made sweet
by Walter, McMahon, Mongo, Iron Mike, Danimal,
the Big O, Buddy, the Colonel, and so many, many
others. A year to be cherished forever as the birth of
a new beginning in Bear Country.